ARTICLES OF WAR

ARTICLES OF WAR

A Collection of American Poetry
about World War II

Edited by Leon Stokesbury

Introduction by Paul Fussell

THE UNIVERSITY OF ARKANSAS PRESS
FAYETTEVILLE   1990   LONDON

Designer: B. J. Zodrow
Typeface: Linotron 202 Goudy Old Style

The paper used in this publication meets the minimum requirements of
the American National Standard for Permanence of Paper for Printed
Library Materials Z39.48-1984. ∞

Library of Congress Cataloging-in-Publication Data

Articles of war : a collection of American poetry about World War II /
    edited by Leon Stokesbury ; introduction by Paul Fussell.
        p.   cm.
    ISBN 1-55728-148-3 (alk. paper). — ISBN 1-55728-149-1 (pbk. :
alk. paper)
    1. American poetry—20th century. 2. World War, 1939–
1945—Poetry. 3. War poetry, American. I. Stokesbury, Leon,
1945– .
PS595.W64A78   1990
811'.54080358—dc20   89-48872
                                                        CIP

Acknowledgments

W. H. AUDEN: "September 1, 1939" copyright 1940 by W. H. Auden. Reprinted from *The English Auden: Poems, Essays and Dramatic Writings*, by W. H. Auden, edited by Edward Mendelson, by permission of Random House, Inc.

DONALD W. BAKER: "Delinquent Elegy" reprinted from *Unposted Letters* by Donald W. Baker. Reprinted by permission of the author.

JOHN BERRYMAN: "The Moon and the Night and the Men" from *Short Poems* by John Berryman. Copyright © 1948 by John Berryman. Reprinted by permission of Farrar, Straus and Giroux, Inc.

DAVID BOTTOMS: "The Anniversary" from *Under the Vulture Tree* by David Bottoms, copyright © 1987 by David Bottoms. Reprinted by permission of William Morrow & Co., Inc.

EDGAR BOWERS: "The Stoic: For Laura Von Courten" reprinted from *Living Together* by Edgar Bowers, reprinted by permission of the author. "Clothes" reprinted by permission of the author.

VAN K. BROCK: "The Behaviorist" and "The Faucets" reprinted by permission of the author.

TURNER CASSITY: "U-24 Anchors off New Orleans (1938)" from *Hurricane Lamp* by Turner Cassity. Reprinted by permission of the University of Chicago Press. Copyright © 1986 by the University of Chicago Press.

JOHN CIARDI: "Return," "Elegy for a Cove Full of Bones," and "Visibility Zero" reprinted by permission from *Saipan: The War Diary of John Ciardi* by John Ciardi, published by The University of Arkansas Press. Copyright Judith Ciardi, 1988. "Sea Burial," "Elegy Just in Case," "On a Photo of Sgt. Ciardi a Year Later," "A Box Comes Home," "V-J Day" reprinted by permission from *Selected Poems* by John Ciardi, published by The University of Arkansas Press. Copyright John Ciardi, 1984.

v

Contents

This book is dedicated to the memory of my father,
Technical Sergeant Leon Burdette Stokesbury (1924–1987),
United States Marine Corps, 1st Division.

For I would be a child to those who mourn
And brother to the foundlings of the field
And friend of innocence and all bright eyes.

—Stanley Kunitz

PREFACE

When I undertook to edit *Articles of War*, I examined the previously published anthologies of World War II war poetry and discovered most contained only British poetry. A smaller number of full collections of American poetry were published, but the most recent of these appeared more than twenty-five years ago. Of the American collections, most were organized thematically, and it was my impression that the anthologies were padded with mediocre verse to fill out the thematic sections and indeed to fill out the anthologies themselves.

As I began reading the American poets of the past fifty years, searching for our best poems on this subject, I quickly realized the truth that Paul Fussell points out in his introduction: with a few significant exceptions, most of the best American poems about World War II were written ex post facto, after the war, and in many cases as long as one or two generations after the war. Today, not only have the poet veterans of the Second World War had ample time to mature as artists, but the poet children of that generation have matured as artists as well. This being so, I decided that the best way to organize the poets in *Articles of War* would be chronologically by date of birth. The anthology begins with a group of poets who were already writing mature work when the war began. It then moves to the major portion of the book, which for the most part includes people who were actual participants in the war, generally as members of the armed forces. The book concludes with poems by a younger generation, some of whom were children during World War II, and finally some who were not born until after the war. My intent is to expose the reader to the full evolving spectrum of American poems about World War II over this last half-century.

Selecting the poems for this book has proven to be an education. I was, of course, aware of the war poems by the best known of the poets in *Articles of War*: Shapiro, Jarrell, Ciardi, Wilbur, Dickey, and Simpson, among others. But there have been more than several welcome personal discoveries. Perhaps the most significant of these are the poems of Lincoln Kirstein and the recent *War Stories* poems of Howard Nemerov. And there were the individual surprises, such as Winfield Townley Scott's "The U.S. Sailor with the Japanese Skull," Edward Field's "World War II," Dorothy Sussman's "River Stories," and P. H. Liotta's "The Story I Can't Tell." What this process has taught me is that the literary accomplishment of the Second World War is immense, and its legacy is brilliant and ongoing. It is my hope that this accomplishment and legacy have been made apparent in *Articles of War*.

I would like to take this opportunity to thank my friend, R. S. Gwynn, for his advice and suggestions as I compiled this collection of poems. Also, I want to thank David Sanders, associate director of the University of Arkansas Press, for his help and many valuable suggestions as well. And finally, great thanks to my wife, Susan Thurman, for once again bearing up under the complications and frustrations that come with an endeavor such as this one. Without the help of these people, this book would be different and less.

Leon Stokesbury

INTRODUCTION

The words *war poetry* seem almost inevitably to suggest the poetry of the First World War, and further, the British poetry of that war, as produced pre-eminently by Wilfred Owen, Isaac Rosenberg, Siegfried Sassoon, and Edmund Blunden. Because the United States entered that war late, suffering only about one-tenth the British casualties (and despite their pep and bravery, more American soldiers died from influenza than from bullets and shells and gas), it is hardly surprising that the American experience then did not occasion a large amount of "war poetry."

Very different was the scene the second time around. Although the British were involved in the Second World War longer than the Americans, by the end the American effort, in Europe as well as the Pacific, was larger than the British, a fact that had less to do with national spirit and values than with such accidents as the greater American population and economic and industrial strength. The literary result this time was a body of war poetry equally British and American in quantity, and in quality as well, with the weight of originality perhaps falling on the American side. This can be said without any disparagement of such British achievements as Henry Reed's "Naming of Parts" and Gavin Ewart's "Officers' Mess" and "When a Beau Goes In." If the continuity of British literary tradition encouraged such distinguished war poets as Keith Douglas,

Alun Lewis, John Pudney, and Vernon Scannell, the Americans came up with Randall Jarrell, Lincoln Kirstein, Richard Eberhart, Karl Shapiro, John Ciardi, Howard Nemerov, Richard Wilbur, James Dickey, and Louis Simpson, many of whom, unlike their British counterparts, built later careers on the foundations of their early war poems. This is notable, because in the First World War it was in fiction rather than poetry that Americans like Hemingway and Dos Passos and Cummings began their literary careers. American poetry somehow drew new life from the Second World War, whose occasions—irony, guilt, horror, black comedy, boredom— seemed to imply themes irresistible to the modern American character. And if in Britain such registrars of the Great War as Robert Graves, Sassoon, and Blunden waited a decade or more before producing the classic memoirs by which that war is remembered, similarly this time many American poets, some too young to have fought, produced their "war poetry" considerably after the war was over. Experience aspiring to assume literary form often benefits from such waiting and ripening, and, for some poets, to peer back at the war through the screen of subsequent events like the assassinations of the Kennedys and Martin Luther King and the scandals of international terrorism and the Vietnam War is to measure the contribution of wartime violence and insensitivity to the tone of contemporary history. W. D. Snodgrass's "'After Experience Taught Me'" and Howard Nemerov's "Redeployment" are examples of what I mean.

At the outset of the Second World War there was little of the enthusiasm that marked the beginning of the First, and there was a conspicuous absence of Rupert Brooke–like verse thanking God for bringing the war to pass and conceiving of the coming experience as really rather jolly, or at least morally good for you. The poets writing out of Hitler's war understood fully how demoralizing it was to be asked to fight the same enemy again after only a twenty-one–year armistice. Quite naturally, this time there was no initial gung-ho poetry of exultation, or even very strenuous patriotism. As Robert E. Sherwood observed, the Second World War was "the first war in American history in which the general disillusionment preceded the firing of the first shot." And that feeling was shared by the Allies in general. As a motive for self-immolation, patriotism now seemed almost obsolete. One Canadian soldier asked, "Who the hell dies for King and Country anymore? That crap went out in the First World War." He enlisted in this one only out of revenge— a friend of his had been killed, and he wanted to kill the killers.

Since the news about the awfulness of modern industrialized war had already been unforgettably delivered by Owen and Sassoon and other poets of the Great War, the poets of the Second War were faced with the question, What is there left to say? Readers who knew the poetry of the earlier war asked their own question: Where are the war poets? In 1943 British poet Keith Douglas observed: "In the fourth year of this war we have not a single poet who seems likely to be an impressive commentator on it." The reason? It's all been said before. As Douglas explains: "Hell cannot be let loose twice. It was let loose in the Great War and it is the same old hell now." Another difficulty for the poet of the Second War was that language seemed now even more debased and unsuitable for the fine discriminations of poetry than in the Great War, when Henry James noted that "The war has used up words: they have weakened, they have deteriorated." As a result of the lies of propaganda and the hyperboles of hate, language suffers, James says, "an increase of limpness." Thus the mode of Second War poetry represents a general skepticism about the former languages of glory and sacrifice and patriotism. Sick of the inflated idiom of official morale-boosting tub-thumping and all the slynesses of wartime publicity and advertising, the poets now preferred to speak in wry understatement, glancing less at the center of a topic than at its edges, proceeding by hints and indirections rather than open, straightforward declaration. As Brian Gardner has said, "A new style emerged: nonchalant, cool, laconic." Finding language so greatly abused in public, some poets could barely bring themselves to deploy it in private. Frederick Ebright, in fact, concluded a poem titled "Memorial to the Great Big Beautiful Self-Sacrificing Advertisers" with the heartfelt line, "There is dignity in silence." And many poets agreed, pursuing a new brevity and minimalism. Randall Jarrell's five-line classic, "The Death of the Ball Turret Gunner," is an example. And a new anonymity is imposed upon characters in poems who earlier might have been carefully named and singled out as heroes. Jarrell significantly withholds the name of the ball turret gunner, just as he seems careful to suggest the multiple, common, and thus vague identities of the characters in his other war poems. On the other hand, writing out of the First World War, E. E. Cummings spent two syllables specifying the name of "Olaf glad and big / whose warmest heart recoiled at war." Now, the wounded soldier in Jarrell's "A Field Hospital" is merely "he," one of ten million identical units from the production line, indistinguishable in their olive drab.

The same suspicion of grandiosity that turns Jarrell away from the gestures of conventional elegy motivates a new kind of poem indigenous to the Second World War, the wry mock-elegy or mock-epitaph whose subject is the self-conscious and embarrassed poet himself. John Ciardi begins his "Elegy Just in Case," "Here lie Ciardi's pearly bones." Indeed, traditional elegy was one of the casualties of the war, despite occasional attempts like Karl Shapiro's "Elegy for a Dead Soldier." More plausible to contemporary readers are such wry, half-apologetic, half-embarrassed glances at the former elegiac mode as Donald W. Baker's "Delinquent Elegy" memorializing one John Smith, a bomber pilot killed with his complete crew when his B-17 crashed on take-off forty years ago. At the time, deaths like that, by meaningless accident, were so routine that, as Baker writes, "no one troubled to sing an elegy / for John Smith and his crew of nine." But now, reminded of the event by seeing some old war movies on late-night TV, Baker pays an obligation possible only now and only in the most unpretentious, understated way:

> I rake old anguish to make my truth
> and record at last some ordinary rhymes,
> a late song for a long-dead youth,
>
> my friend John Smith, who, in the Second War,
> blew up and burned, one among many,
> a clownish hero, killed by error,
> as smart as most, as brave as any.

That world of thousand-plane bomber raids on civilians is light-years away from the First World War of rifles and machine-guns in the trenches, and its poetry must be expected to be radically different too. The Second War was worldwide, ranging from the sweat of the South Pacific to the frozen feet of the Belgian winter, embracing machines operating fifty thousand feet above the sea to other machines operating hundreds of feet below it. This war was almost unimaginably multitudinous, involving hundreds of millions and killing or wounding over seventy-eight million, more of them civilians than soldiers, including nearly six million Jews beaten, shot, or gassed to death by the Germans. Eight hundred was the number of divisions mustered by the Soviets to repel the German invasion, and, at the battle of Kursk in 1943, two million soldiers were engaged, together with six thousand tanks and four thousand planes.

This war featured also such hard-to-believe artifacts as landing craft, booby traps, anti-tank mines, barrage balloons, and self-propelled bombs and rockets designed not to damage troops but to terrorize civilians. And the war featured as well such hitherto unfamiliar behavior as the willingness of Japanese troops to kill themselves, whether on the ground or in kamikaze planes, an indication of a new manic desperation in war which taxed the interpretative powers not just of poets but of virtually everyone. Madness was abroad, and the poets as well as others confronted the difficulty of making sense, moral or artistic, out of behavior so remote from former civilized norms. Barbara Foley has defined the problem while commenting on the Holocaust. It's not, she notes, that its data are "unknowable." The impediment to understanding the Holocaust, like the impediment to the poets' artistic understanding of the war, is that "its full dimensions are inaccessible to the ideological frameworks we have inherited from the liberal era."

And it might be easy to overlook another cause of the uniqueness of this body of poetry. It was written, most of it, during the very high tide of "modernism," with that movement's suspicion of romantic emotion in poetry and its reliance on irony as an insulating material. Hence we find here irony in plenty, from the sentimental sort purveyed by Phyllis McGinley to the maturer kind in Miller Williams and Peter Viereck and Richard Wilbur. Viereck and Wilbur imply how different this poetry is going to be from that of earlier wars, for both find a terrible irony in the "planting" of the anti-tank and anti-personnel mines, unique to this war, in the midst of the flora which used to be the very stuff of poetry. There is new cunning and cruelty and technological skill and insensate wickedness and a modern literary anti-pastoralism all betokened at once in Viereck's "Ripeness Is All," in which

> Gardeners in boots
> Plant tender seeds of mines
> Where the dimmed flashlight shines,
> Nursing the wire-vines,
> Hiding the roots.

And in "Mined Country," Wilbur contemplates the horror to persist long after the war when the buried mines, many overlooked in the general fear and haste, explode when touched by innocent country people:

Danger is sunk in the pastures, the woods are sly,
Ingenuity's covered with flowers!

. . .

Shepherds must learn a new language; this
Isn't going to be quickly solved.

Another unprecedented kind of poem is the aerial bombing or bomber-crew poem, as written by Ciardi, Richard Hugo, Dickey, Edgar Bowers, Edward Field, P. H. Liotta, and Jarrell. Guilt at murdering civilians is often either text or sub-text here, and in "Eighth Air Force," Jarrell eases the moral problem by invoking that rare object of allusion in Second World War poetry, the New Testament—here, Pilate's words about the innocence of Jesus, "I find no fault in this just man." And there is irony too, and also of a novel kind, in the lurking home-front secret anti-Semitism of people formally enrolled in a struggle to the death against foreign anti-Semitism. That is what William Trowbridge dramatizes in "Home Front," where Cousin Bob, his son destroyed in a bombing raid on Germany, sits in his porch swing alternately trying to figure out what it has all meant and ridiculing the oddities of the local Jews, who, he seems to feel, are somehow implicated as cause and rationale of all this unrestrained death and destruction. In the poems focusing on the cruel work of the B-17s, fear, a topic virtually untouched in earlier war poetry, is confronted frankly, and fear, unmentionable in most of the poems associated with the First World War, now comes into its own. Lincoln Kirstein is brilliant at registering fear in a demotic, twisted soldier's idiom thoroughly convincing, just as he triumphs also in his portrayals of wartime boredom, chickenshit, criminality among the troops, and general absurdity—all poetic themes largely unexplored before this new war brought them to the attention of unprecedented multitudes.

Even if they don't read a great deal of poetry, those who were in the war, either at the front or at home, will feel, reading these poems, an uncanny shock of recognition. Soldiers especially will be astonished at the vividness with which these poems bring it all back: the humiliations of the physical exam; the new-wood smell of the barracks, and the over-chlorinated water; the boring training and the exhausting disciplinary marches in alarming heat and cold; the empty-minded waiting in interminable lines—for chow, for injections, for issue of equipment; the pain and tenseness; the shortage of subtle, precious, tender, and beautiful things; the endless trips on troop trains, and the bone-wracking rides in 2½-ton trucks; the letters from home, and from girls, overflowing with love and innocence; the pass and shore-leave towns, with their cynical bars and bad restaurants and military-supply shops and whores; the crowding and vomit of the troop transport. And later, the crack of bullets and shells; the unmanning fear; the sadism directed at the enemy; and wounds and the amputations and the dead bodies. The constant longing for it to be over, and the inexpressible joy when it finally was over. And readers who did not experience those things can learn here what a number of extraordinarily intelligent, sensitive, and articulate observers made of it all.

Paul Fussell

ARTICLES OF WAR

ROBINSON JEFFERS

(1887–1962)

Pearl Harbor

I

Here are the fireworks. The men who conspired and labored
To embroil this republic in the wreck of Europe have got their
    bargain—
And a bushel more. As for me, what can I do but fly the national
    flag from the top of the tower?
America has neither race nor religion nor its own language: nation
    or nothing.
                        Stare, little tower,
Confidently across the Pacific, the flag on your head. I built you at
    the other war's end,
And the sick peace; I based you on living rock, granite on granite;
    I said, "Look, you gray stones:
Civilization is sick: stand awhile and be quiet and drink the sea-
    wind, you will survive
Civilization."
                        But now I am old, and O stones be modest. Look,
    little tower:
This dust blowing is only the British Empire; these torn leaves
    flying
Are only Europe; the wind is the plane-propellers; the smoke is
    Tokyo. The child with the butchered throat
Was too young to be named. Look no farther ahead.

II

The war that we have carefully for years provoked
Catches us unprepared, amazed and indignant. Our warships are
    shot

Like sitting ducks and our planes like nest-birds, both our coasts
    ridiculously panicked,
And our leaders make orations. This is the people
That hopes to impose on the whole planetary world
An American peace.
                  (Oh, we'll not lose our war: my money on
    amazed Gulliver
And his horse-pistols.)
                         Meanwhile our prudent officers
Have cleared the coast-long ocean of ships and fishingcraft, the
    sky of planes, the windows of light: these clearings
Make a great beauty. Watch the wide sea; there is nothing human;
    its gulls have it. Watch the wide sky
All day clean of machines; only at dawn and dusk one military
    hawk passes
High on patrol. Walk at night in the black-out,
The firefly lights that used to line the long shore
Are all struck dumb; shut are the shops, mouse-dark the houses.
    Here the prehuman dignity of night
Stands, as it was before and will be again. O beautiful
Darkness and silence, the two eyes that see God; great staring
    eyes.

MARIANNE MOORE
(1887–1972)

In Distrust of Merits

Strengthened to live, strengthened to die for
  medals and positioned victories?
They're fighting, fighting, fighting the blind
  man who thinks he sees—
who cannot see that the enslaver is
enslaved; the hater, harmed. O shining O
  firm star, O tumultuous
    ocean lashed till small things go
    as they will, the mountainous
      wave makes us who look, know

depth. Lost at sea before they fought! O
  star of David, star of Bethlehem,
O black imperial lion
  of the Lord—emblem
of a risen world—be joined at last, be
joined. There is hate's crown beneath which all is
    death; there's love's without which none
      is king; the blessed deeds bless
      the halo. As contagion
        of sickness makes sickness,

contagion of trust can make trust. They're
  fighting in deserts and caves, one by
one, in battalions and squadrons;
  they're fighting that I
may yet recover from the disease, My
Self; some have it lightly; some will die. "Man's
    wolf to man" and we devour
      ourselves. The enemy could not

have made a greater breach in our
defenses. One pilot-

ing a blind man can escape him, but
Job disheartened by false comfort knew
that nothing can be so defeating
as a blind man who
can see. O alive who are dead, who are
proud not to see, O small dust of the earth
that walks so arrogantly,
trust begets power and faith is
an affectionate thing. We
vow, we make this promise

to the fighting—it's a promise—"We'll
never hate black, white, red, yellow, Jew,
Gentile, Untouchable." We are
not competent to
make our vows. With set jaw they are fighting,
fighting, fighting—some we love whom we know,
some we love but know not—that
hearts may feel and not be numb.
It cures me; or am I what
I can't believe in? Some

in snow, some on crags, some in quicksands,
little by little, much by much, they
are fighting fighting fighting that where
there was death there may
be life. "When a man is prey to anger,
he is moved by outside things; when he holds
his ground in patience patience
patience, that is action or
beauty," the soldier's defense
and hardest armor for

the fight. The world's an orphans' home. Shall
we never have peace without sorrow?
without pleas of the dying for
help that won't come? O
quiet form upon the dust, I cannot

look and yet I must. If these great patient
  dyings—all these agonies
    and wound-bearings and bloodshed—
    can teach us how to live, these
    dyings were not wasted.

Hate-hardened heart, O heart of iron,
  iron is iron till it is rust.
There never was a war that was
  not inward; I must
fight till I have conquered in myself what
causes war, but I would not believe it.
  I inwardly did nothing.
    O Iscariot-like crime!
  Beauty is everlasting
    and dust is for a time.

Archibald MacLeish

(1892–1982)

The Young Dead Soldiers

for Lieutenant Richard Myers

The young dead soldiers do not speak.
Nevertheless, they are heard in the still houses: who has not heard
    them?
They have a silence that speaks for them at night and when the
    clock counts.
They say: We were young. We have died. Remember us.
They say: We have done what we could but until it is finished it is
    not done.
They say: We have given our lives but until it is finished no one
    can know what our lives gave.
They say: Our deaths are not ours; they are yours; they will mean
    what you make them.
They say: Whether our lives and our deaths were for peace and a
    new hope or for nothing we cannot say; it is you who must
    say this.
They say: We leave you our deaths. Give them their meaning.
We were young, they say. We have died. Remember us.

E. E. CUMMINGS
(1894-1962)

plato told

him:he couldn't
believe it(jesus

told him;he
wouldn't believe
it)lao

tsze
certainly told
him,and general
(yes

mam)
sherman;
and even
(believe it
or

not)you
told him:i told
him;we told him
(he didn't believe it,no

sir)it took
a nipponized bit of
the old sixth

avenue
el;in the top of his head:to tell

him

RICHARD EBERHART

(1904–)

The Fury of Aerial Bombardment

You would think the fury of aerial bombardment
Would rouse God to relent; the infinite spaces
Are still silent. He looks on shock-pried faces.
History, even, does not know what is meant.

You would feel that after so many centuries
God would give man to repent; yet he can kill
As Cain could, but with multitudinous will,
No farther advanced than in his ancient furies.

Was man made stupid to see his own stupidity?
Is God by definition indifferent, beyond us all?
Is the eternal truth man's fighting soul
Wherein the Beast ravens in its own avidity?

Of Van Wettering I speak, and Averill,
Names on a list, whose faces I do not recall
But they are gone to early death, who late in school
Distinguished the belt feed lever from the belt holding pawl.

Phyllis McGinley

(1905–1978)

The Portents

"Trial blackout of city studied by officials."
—Headline in the New York Times.

By a cloud, by rings on the moon
Or a bough that casts no shadow,
By the snowflake falling at noon
In a shriveled meadow
Do the knowing eye and the reason
Predict the season.

So who can regard the least
Of these things with pulse untroubled?
The wind has veered to the east,
The fields are stubbled,
And the shrewd airs inform
Us of the storm.

Whose hands—not yours, not mine—
Shall hold the floods in tether?
We have seen the cloud and the sign,
But we cannot stay the weather.
Run to your house. Pull fast
Your shutters on the blast.

Though there is no safety there,
I think. Nor anywhere.

Soldier Asleep

Soldier asleep, and stirring in your sleep,
In tent, trench, dugout, foxhole, or swampy slough,
I pray the Lord your rifle and soul to keep,
And your body, too,

From the hid sniper in the leafy tangle,
From shrapnel, from the barbed and merciless wire,
From tank, from bomb, from the booby trap in the jungle,
From water, from fire.

It was an evil wind that blew you hither,
Soldier, to this strange bed—
A tempest brewed from the world's malignant weather.

Safe may you sleep, instead,
Once more in the room with the pennants tacked on the wall,
Or the room in the bachelor apartment, 17 L,
The club room, the furnished room across the hall,
The room in the cheap hotel,

The double-decker at home, the bench in the park,
The attic cot, the hammock under the willow,
Or the wide bed in the remembered dark
With the belovèd's head beside you on the pillow.

Safe may the winds return you to the place
That, howsoever it was, was better than this.

V-Day

Savor the hour as it comes. Preserve it in amber.
  Instruct the mind to cherish its sound and its shape.
Cut out the newspaper clippings. Forever remember
  The horns and the ticker tape,

The flags, the parades, the radio talking and talking,
  Ceaselessly crying the tale on the noisy air
(But omitting for once the commercials), the sirens shrieking,
  The bulletins in Times Square,

The women kneeling in churches, the people's laughter,
  The speeches, the rumors, the tumult loud in the street.
Remember it shrewdly so you can say hereafter,
  "That moment was safe and sweet.

"Safe was the day and the world was safe for living,
  For Democracy, Liberty, all of the coin-bright names.
Were not the bomb bays empty, the tanks unmoving,
  The cities no more in flames?

"That was an island in time, secure and candid,
  When we seemed to walk in freedom as in the sun,
With a promise kept, with the dangers of battle ended,
  And the fearful perils of peace not yet begun."

Ballad of Fine Days

"Temperatures have soared to almost
summer levels . . . making conditions
ideal for bombing offensives."
—Excerpt from B. B. C. news
broadcast.

All in the summery weather,
  To east and south and north,
The bombers fly together
  And the fighters squire them forth.

While the lilac bursts in flower
  And buttercups brim with gold,
Hour by lethal hour,
  Now fiercer buds unfold.

For the storms of springtime lessen,
  The meadow lures the bee,
And there blooms tonight in Essen
  What bloomed in Coventry.

All in the summery weather,
  Fleeter than swallows fare,
The bombers fly together
  Through the innocent air.

Landscape without Figures

The shape of the summer has not changed at all.
There is no difference in the sky's rich color,
In texture of cloud or leaf or languid hill.
The fringed wave is no duller.

Even the look of this village does not change—
Shady and full of gardens and near the sea.
But something is lacking. Something sad and strange
Troubles the memory.

Where are they?—the boys, not children and not men,
In polo shirts or jeans or autographed blazers,
With voices suddenly deep, and proud on each chin
The mark of new razors.

They were workers or players, but always the town was theirs.
They wiped your windshield, they manned the parking lots.
They delivered your groceries. They drove incredible cars
As if they were chariots.

They were the lifeguards, self-conscious, with little whistles.
They owned the tennis courts and the Saturday dances.
They were barbarous-dark with sun. They were vain of their
      muscles
And the girls' glances.

They boasted, and swam, and lounged at the drugstore's portal.
They sailed their boats and carried new records down.
They never took thought but that they were immortal,
And neither did the town.

But now they are gone like leaves, like leaves in the fall,
Though the shape of the summer has not changed at all.

The Mixture as Before

Summer is icumen in,
   Sound the sirens, light the torches,
Warn the roses to begin
   Climbing up suburban porches.
Let the laurel run like fire
   Over all the upland reaches
But be wary of the wire,
   Barbed and bright, along the beaches.

Hark! The blithe, the morning bird,
   Early singing, stirs our slumber
Where the young man, undeferred,
   Waits upon his legal number.
Now the wren's unmortgaged nest
   Hugs our hospitable acre,
And the ski pole takes its rest
   With the rationed Studebaker.

Now the sails of summer fill,
   Now the waves are all a-glimmer,
Though attentive at his drill
   Stands the lean and sunburnt swimmer.
Now the lilies swoon with sun,
   Now the cricket pipes the shadows
And the anti-aircraft gun
   Crouches in astonished meadows.

Here is June. So let the ice
   Tinkle in unsweetened glasses.
Fling the immemorial rice.
   Strew the picnic on the grasses.
Tell the chattering mind to hush
   For one soft, deceptive hour
While the berry fires the bush
   And the bee invades the flower,

Till in lupine-colored light
  Dusk dissolves, the stars are certain,
And the aromatic night
  Leans against the blackout curtain.

W. H. AUDEN

(1907–1973)

September 1, 1939

I sit in one of the dives
On Fifty-second Street
Uncertain and afraid
As the clever hopes expire
Of a low dishonest decade:
Waves of anger and fear
Circulate over the bright
And darkened lands of the earth,
Obsessing our private lives;
The unmentionable odour of death
Offends the September night.

Accurate scholarship can
Unearth the whole offence
From Luther until now
That has driven a culture mad,
Find what occurred at Linz,
What huge imago made
A psychopathic god:
I and the public know
What all schoolchildren learn,
Those to whom evil is done
Do evil in return.

Exiled Thucydides knew
All that a speech can say
About Democracy,
And what dictators do,
The elderly rubbish they talk
To an apathetic grave;

Analysed all in his book,
The enlightenment driven away,
The habit-forming pain,
Mismanagement and grief:
We must suffer them all again.

Into this neutral air
Where blind skyscrapers use
Their full height to proclaim
The strength of Collective Man,
Each language pours its vain
Competitive excuse:
But who can live for long
In an euphoric dream;
Out of the mirror they stare,
Imperialism's face
And the international wrong.

Faces along the bar
Cling to their average day:
The lights must never go out,
The music must always play,
All the conventions conspire
To make this fort assume
The furniture of home;
Lest we should see where we are,
Lost in a haunted wood,
Children afraid of the night
Who have never been happy or good.

The windiest militant trash
Important Persons shout
Is not so crude as our wish:
What mad Nijinsky wrote
About Diaghilev
Is true of the normal heart;
For the error bred in the bone
Of each woman and each man
Craves what it cannot have,
Not universal love
But to be loved alone.

From the conservative dark
Into the ethical life
The dense commuters come,
Repeating their morning vow;
"I *will* be true to the wife,
I'll concentrate more on my work,"
And helpless governors wake
To resume their compulsory game:
Who can release them now,
Who can reach the deaf,
Who can speak for the dumb?

All I have is a voice
To undo the folded lie,
The romantic lie in the brain
Of the sensual man-in-the-street
And the lie of Authority
Whose buildings grope the sky:
There is no such thing as the State
And no one exists alone;
Hunger allows no choice
To the citizen or the police;
We must love one another or die.

Defenceless under the night
Our world in stupor lies;
Yet, dotted everywhere,
Ironic points of light
Flash out wherever the Just
Exchange their messages:
May I, composed like them
Of Eros and of dust,
Beleaguered by the same
Negation and despair,
Show an affirming flame.

LINCOLN KIRSTEIN
(1907–)

Rank

Differences between rich and poor, king and queen,
Cat and dog, hot and cold, day and night, now and then,
Are less clearly distinct than all those between
Officers and us: enlisted men.

Not by brass may you guess nor their private latrine
Since distinctions obtain in any real well-run war;
It's when off duty, drunk, one acts nice or mean
In a sawdust-strewn bistro-type bar.

Ours was on a short street near the small market square;
Farmers dropped by for some beer or oftener to tease
The Gargantuan bartender Jean-Pierre
About his sweet wife, Marie-Louise.

GI's got the habit who liked French movies or books,
Tried to talk French or were happy to be left alone;
It was our kinda club; we played chess in nooks
With the farmers. We made it our own.

To this haven one night came an officer bold; .
Crocked and ugly, he'd had it in five bars before.
A lurid luster glazed his eye which foretold
He'd better stay out of our shut door,

But did not. He barged in, slung his cap on the zinc:
"Dewbelle veesky," knowing well there was little but beer.
Jean-Pierre showed the list of what one could drink:
"What sorta jerk joint you running here?"

Jean-Pierre had wine but no whisky to sell.
Wine loves the soul. Hard liquor hots up bloody fun,
And it's our rule noncommissioned personnel
Must keep by them their piece called a gun.

As well we are taught, enlisted soldiers may never
Ever surrender this piece—M1, carbine, or rifle—
With which no mere officer whomsoever
May freely or foolishly trifle.

A porcelain stove glowed in its niche, white and warm.
Jean-Pierre made jokes with us French-speaking boys.
Marie-Louise lay warm in bed far from harm;
Upstairs, snored through the ensuing noise.

This captain swilled beer with minimal grace. He began:
"Shit. What you-all are drinkin's not liquor. It's piss."
Two privates (first class) now consider some plan
To avoid what may result from this.

Captain Stearnes is an Old Army joe. Eighteen years
In the ranks, man and boy; bad luck, small promotion;
Without brains or cash, not the cream of careers.
Frustration makes plenty emotion.

"Now, Mac," Stearnes grins (Buster's name is not Mac; it is Jack),
"Toss me your gun an' I'll show you an old army trick;
At forty feet, with one hand, I'll crack that stove, smack."
"Let's not," drawls Jack back, scared of this prick.

"You young punk," Stearnes now storms, growing moody but
        mean,
"Do you dream I daren't pull my superior rank?"
His hand snatches Jack's light clean bright carbine.
What riddles the roof is no blank.

The rifle is loaded as combat zones ever require.
His arm kicks back without hurt to a porcelain stove.
Steel drilling plaster and plank, thin paths of fire
Plug Marie-Louise sleeping above.

Formal enquiry subsequent to this shootin'
Had truth and justice separately demanded.
Was Stearnes found guilty? You are darned tootin':
Fined, demoted. More: reprimanded.

The charge was not murder, mayhem, mischief malicious,
Yet something worse, and this they brought out time and again:
Clearly criminal and caddishly vicious
Was his: Drinking With Enlisted Men.

I'm serious. It's what the Judge Advocate said:
Strict maintenance of rank or our system is sunk.
Stearnes saluted. Jean-Pierre wept his dead.
Jack and I got see-double drunk.

Foresight

Previsioning death in advance, our doom is delayed.
I guess mine:
I'm driving for some dumb officer on this raid:

I can't doubt his sense of direction, his perfect right.
Still, he's wrong.
I hint we're too far front. Been warned plenty about this before.

Base far off. No lights may be shown. He starts to get sore.
Lost, our road.
He feels he's failed. Abruptly down drops night.

Anticipate panic: his, mine, contagions fear takes.
THIS IS IT.
Not good. I invoke calm plus prayer for both our sakes.

Calm makes sense. Prayer is less useful than gin or a smoke.
Where are we?
If this ass hadn't tried to crack his great big joke,

Pushing beyond where he knew well we were told to go,
We'd be safe.
Checking my estimate, my unvoiced I Told You So,

Granite bang-bangs blossom all over hell and gone.
Let me Out!
My foreseen fright swells, a warm swarm and we're sure done

In by Mistake, including his fright, faking him brave;
Me the same,
Making me clam tight when I oughta had the brains to save

Our skins, sparing official pride by baring my fear:
(Please, sir. *Turn.*)
Sharing his shame with me, who, also, deserve some. Oh dear,

It's too late. The end of two nervous careers,
Of dear me,
And him, dear doubtless to someone, worth her dear tears.

Vet

A tired new trooper scans the beach
  Where but some twenty dawns before
He, with those thousands of his force,
  Barely achieved this shallow shore.

Through hip-high water over flats
  Gritty cross fire cracked its knife;
Aching blasts sucked all the air
  From quick collapsing sacks of life.

Here where near-misses lapped his craft
  Landings by dozens scar the sand;
There where scratched-off bombers plunged
  Beetle-boats swarm the busy strand.

Across the bay, blunt puffs of smoke;
  A war seems somewhere—miles from here.
He feels its desultory bang:
  Land mines blown by engineers.

Just three weeks after our great act
  He can't recall half his own wild
Sobbing advance. High on a dune,
  This prematurely aging child,

A mite of history he helped make,
  Rubs stubble chin, and spends a sigh.
Tomorrow he'll be down the line
  Waiting one more chance to die.

Guts

In its seat 'twixt bowel and bladder
Sits the nerve that insists he must dance.
Now he's tense, but what surly disaster
Might mar him a clean pair of pants?
No sense in anticipation;
When it comes, the man says, it sure comes.
This world holds small harvest of heroes
In its gross annual crop of sly crumbs.
Louse he is, but sustains the slim notion
Salvaging him even from fear,
Like curiosity, subtle emotion,
More selfless than first might appear.

When he was a big boy in britches
He got a girl in his daddy's sedan.
It was also the first time for her and
Almost over before it began.
Before he undid she was bloody;
What happened before he was in?
She was only paying her monthly
Wages to original sin.

He should have stopped there but he did not.
Was it courage compelled him to crime?
He was new, hot, hard; and he wanted
To savor the treasure of time.
Bathed in lamb's blood, dried on lamb's wool,
Baptized Buster becomes him a man.
The spunk to buck distaste or habit
Learns you more than a good high-school can.

In a farmer's field five miles from Nancy,
On a dark winter morn, '44.
I drove back alone from Thionville
To Third Army Headquarters Corps.

27

This here field ploughed with raw furrows
In swipes of wide violent earth:
Two medium tanks held disputation
On the essence of death and rebirth.
On its slung treads one tank was flipped over,
The other a crushed can of beer—
Two beetles squashed on their cat-tracks,
Me the one live thing anywhere near.

I parked my vehicle by the roadside,
Pursued tank tracks o'er the spoiled snow;
Implored my morale to quit stalling
Till I'd probed the fierce fate of a foe.

It was rather richer in bloodshed
Than the lass in my daddy's sedan.
You can feature what can't help but happen
When fire grills a thin-armored can,
Such container containing live persons
Who'd climbed in as enlisted men.
If you think this pageant smelled holy
Then you can say that again.

One question, one answer, acquits us;
Caught cheating, we only confess:
"Who the hell do you think you are, man?"
"No worse than that bloody mess."
They're dead and I'm living: it's nonsense.
They're shattered; I'm whole: it's a lie.
Between us, identification:
I am you, men; and, men, you are I.
Tests of failure, dishonor can hardly
Be matters of all-out degree.
Fresh earth will smother you sweetly;
A warm bath can take care of me.
Gruesome glimpses we stare down, maintain us,
Sin and squalor partly appeased.
Such scale bravery may even sustain us,
Our psyches released or increased.
We've endured the Worst That Can Happen.
Hallelujah! There can't be much more,

But the ghastly surprises of history
Hide their inexhaustible store,
And exams in a peace that we pray for
Make dunces of scholars at war.

Interpreter

In her cold, unlighted piece
   Six flights above the street
She's pinned by us inquisitors
   Who brutally repeat
Questions she's already sworn
   Answers she doesn't know.
But that was to their dull police
   While we are different, though
We have our style of charm quite like
   Her friend, a Francophile;
Both of us are generous
   With cigarette and guile.
My captain speaks no French. He feels
   Futile in his distress;
He formulates a foolish trap
   Which even he must guess
May never net so sly a doe:
   "Ask her," he orders me,
"Was she—intimate—with this joe?"
   And she: "What's intimacy?"
"Well, did she have—goddam it, man—
   Relations with this kid?"
"*Bien. Relations . . . on peut dire.*"
   So try again we did.
"If what you mean is what I think"—
   She frowns; her cigarette
Has smouldered out and she won't ask
   For another one just yet—
"Why, yes. He's sweet. I like him well.
   And what is wrong with that?"
Stretches, yawns, purrs, spreads herself
   To curl, a svelte house-cat.
Commands my captain: "Ask her more,"
   But senses his defeat,
So after further feeble jabs
   We issue to the street.

My captain never will confide
    In this enlisted dough;
Aside from rude conjecture I
    May never really know
What's here involved; what these kids did,
    Who caught more than a kiss
Though on some profounder plane
    There's nothing much to miss.
Six tall flights up, the pretty puss
    Leans at her windowpane,
Idly wondering which of us
    Will scale her stairs again.

Patton

Skirting a scrub-pine forest there's a scent of snow in air;
Scattered sentries in smart combat dress accord us their sharp
    stare;
My chaplain for the first time now allows as where we are:
    At the core of this campaign.

Detroit's vast ingenuity subsumes our plans for doom,
Commandeers an auto-trailer to serve as a map-room;
Hermetic and impersonal, one may reasonably assume
    This is Third Army's brain.

I spy a female nurse pass by, baiting a white bull-pup,
Official pet of General's and a humane cover-up
For isolated living or affection's leaky cup
    At secret headquarters.

Nurse accepts my chaplain's solemn amateur salute;
He lets the pup lick and sniff his shiny combat boot,
Shoots her a semiprecious smile which all agree is cute—
    Raps on that map-room door.

Should I from sloppy jeep jump out and to attention snap?
Patton's informal entrance seems some sort of booby trap,
But his easy stoic manner is devoid of any crap,
    So I stick right in my car.

Measuring our morality or elegance in war,
I marked our nurse compose herself. Starch-white, she primly wore
A gold-filled heart-shaped locket on her chest, and this was for
    Second, minute, hour.

Time's analysis is portable and only time can tell
What's in the works for all of us—nurse, chaplain, general.
Syllables in separate hour, minute, second, simply spell
    Military power.

Our brass cut short their conference, and Patton turns to me:
"Well, soldier, how about a cup of hot delicious tea?
Unless I am mistaken, Nurse may even add whisky."
        "Oh, thank you, sir," I said.

"Chaplain says you come from Boston. Then you know it is my
        home;
Now both of us are many miles from Bulfinch's golden dome.
By springtime it is where I hope the both of us may come
        Provided we ain't dead."

Nurse's watch ticked its temporal tune. Chaplain and I returned
To our base of operations whilst vict'ries blazed and burned.
Reckless Patton's vehicle one year later overturned:
        I see him as a saint.

Angels who flanked his final fling to martial glory's niche
Named Lucifer as honor guard, for that son of a bitch
My immortal captain's mortal, and also he touched pitch;
        His stars tarnished from taint.

In *Stars & Stripes* we read it when he slapped that soldier down
Cringing in a psycho-ward to play the coward clown,
Presuming to a state of shock (he'd smashed a stubborn town),
        But Patton blew his stack.

For me and my companions whom slap and shock stung too
Though minimal responsible find other factors true:
The pathos in enlisted men's not special to the few;
        It is the generals' lack.

Inspecting cots of amputees, unshaken obviously,
Approves the stitch above the wrist, the slice below the knee;
Hides in th' enlisted men's latrine so he can quietly
        Have one good hearty cry.

This soldier has to take a leak, finds someone sobbing there.
To my horror it's an officer; his stars make this quite clear.
I gasp: "Oh, sir; are you all right?" Patton grumbles: "Fair.
        Something's in my eye."

With vict'ry's brittle climax pity's never far away;
Patton feels only wounds should hurt which help him win the day.
But wounds have casual exits and it's often hard to say
    If blood flows in or out.

When endowed as a fine artist you can fling the paint around;
Or, called to seek salvation, you can make a solemn sound.
But crafty priestlike soldiers keep one premise as their ground:
    Loose fright ends up as rout.

Patton's a combat artist; hence his palette runs to red;
Makes superior generals anxious he's prone to lose his head,
Spoil pretty Rhenish landscapes with an April coat of lead:
    Our man may go too far.

The British and Canadians are ordered to push through;
Patton learns he's just their anchor with nothing much to do
But cultivate impatience, curse and sweat or curse and stew—
    Not his concept of war.

He vows: "Now you go fuck yourselves. I'm taking off from here."
He vanishes, nor hide nor hair. At SHAEF there is grave fear.
They bid him halt; he wires 'em straight: "I HAVE JUST TAKEN
    TRIER,
    SO SHALL I GIVE IT BACK?"

Military governor, Bavaria's shattered state,
He had a naïve notion which was not so all-fired great;
Hired him all former Nazis who'd nicely coöperate.
    For this he gets the sack.

And yet—it's not entirely fair. Since war is done and won,
Patton fears peace as idleness, peacetime as seldom fun;
Idleness is devil's business, and for the devil's son
    Good Nazis don't rank least.

This old pro was an innocent. Thank Christ for simple souls,
Pearl pistol-packin' poppa, prince of polo's thousand goals,
And I'm not fooling you, my friend: he starred three major rôles:
    Warrior, craftsman, priest.

We were rained right out of Nancy. Firm Metz we could not free.
Floods muddied fields; his bogged-down tanks less use than
    cavalry;
Came his orders: ALL PERSONNEL WILL PRAY THAT THESE UNSEA-
SONABLE RAINS SHALL CEASE.

George Patton through proper channels forwards his request.
There comes logical reply to logistical behest;
Who am I to testify it's some joker's sorry jest?
    Rains cease. His tanks make peace.

Hijack

We drive all day from mildly picturesque Coumbes-sur-Seine
Through impressionist landscape it's nice to be seeing again;
My colonel, no companion of choice, uncorks his private pint
    of pain.

I've driven for this old pre–World-War-I crock before.
He doesn't like me for stink; I deem him a snobby old bore;
But we're inextricably linked by certain tensions ingrained in
    this war.

His grief derives from a grandson he's crazy about
Whom he's learned was captured two days ago in a censored rout
Of U.S. troops. Now we ride up front fast trying to find something
    out.

North, ever north; then northeast. Disturbing tableaux abound—
Relics of men and machinery, busted husks tossed around.
As we roll through sinister buzzings, nervous-making mysterious
    sound

Upsets us and—bang—we stall in a small market square—
But how best to describe it? A pitched battle takes place right
    there
While the parties engaged wear one uniform: ours. Interpret this
    scare

As some insane gag, but now a big gasoline truck
Overturns. Jerry-cans bounce on fierce combatants striking or
    struck
By fist, gun butt, monkey wrench. If we have only average luck

Things won't pop, someone get hurt: us. I watch Colonel stand
In our dead jeep shouting orders, though none obey his command
Sensible as it sounds: "Stop, boys; stop right now," and then his
    good right hand

Reaches for side arms. I yank him down, jerk our jeep back.
Bodies swivel around the vehicle and dusk dyes to deep black
While it all gets more unreal although staying real enough.
    Absolute lack

Of discipline or authority. Colonel slumps down
Sulking through this crazy vague riot in a French border town
Where American soldiers sock one another for some obscure
    renown.

Hence: construe this authentic hilarious scene,
Melodramatic yet stereoscopic. What has just been
Logical chaos stems from hysteria mainly about gasoline.

Our motorized units forged so wildly far ahead
Many imagined they'd seized victory but were then stopped dead.
Whichever eager beaver planned this mad push should have stood
    in bed.

Hence we hijack gas from whom gas has to hijack;
There's nowhere near enough to make up our present serious lack,
Not alone to sustain an advance but to stop being shoved way back.

Colonel and I, in sort of a bad spot, are safe enough.
I still have, thank Christ, my own tank half full of the sacred stuff,
Which brings us back to base though driving blackout routes by
    night is rough.

My pre–World-War-I officer sweats in the dirt
Clinging to a great American army losing its lousy shirt—
His adored grandson captured by the enemy; lost, maybe
    hurt. . . .

Tent-mates

It's no cinch to live together
    In a field three acres square
With your noncoms and your officers
    Sleeping and eating there.
Soldiers aren't chosen wisely
    To be four-season friends;
Neither lovers nor companions,
    We were picked for rougher ends.
Hence our interest seems to lessen
    In snapshots of buddies' wives,
Nor are we all-absorbed by
    Incidents in lurid lives
Which startlingly resemble
    Our own grim or comic tale
But which, on other lips than ours,
    In passion tend to pale.
From living in each other's laps,
    From sniffing at each other's pores,
From glimpsing every function of
    The human mechanism's chores,
From dozing next to unloved flesh,
    From swimming in the common stew,
We're trigger happy to the touch
    At our compulsive rendezvous.
I do not mind my own shit.
    Why then avoid another's?
Answers are articles of war:
    Men are seldom brothers.

WINFIELD TOWNLEY SCOTT
(1910–1968)

The U.S. Sailor with the Japanese Skull

Bald-bare, bone-bare, and ivory yellow: skull
Carried by a thus two-headed U.S. sailor
Who got it from a Japanese soldier killed
At Guadalcanal in the ever-present war: our

Bluejacket, I mean, aged 20, in August strolled
Among the little bodies on the sand and hunted
Souvenirs: teeth, tags, diaries, boots; but bolder still
Hacked off this head and under a Ginkgo tree skinned it:

Peeled with a lifting knife the jaw and cheeks, bared
The nose, ripped off the black-haired scalp and gutted
The dead eyes to these thoughtful hollows: a scarred
But bloodless job, unless it be said brains bleed.

Then, his ship underway, dragged this aft in a net
Many days and nights—the cold bone tumbling
Beneath the foaming wake, weed-worn and salt-cut
Rolling safe among fish and washed with Pacific;

Till on a warm and level-keeled day hauled in
Held to the sun and the sailor, back to a gun-rest,
Scrubbed the cured skull with lye, perfecting this:
Not foreign as he saw it first: death's familiar cast.

Bodiless, fleshless, nameless, it and the sun
Offend each other in strange fascination
As though one of the two were mocked; but nothing is in
This head, or it fills with what another imagines

As: here were love and hate and the will to deal
Death or to kneel before it, death emperor,
Recorded orders without reasons, bomb-blast, still
A child's morning, remembered moonlight on Fujiyama:

All scoured out now by the keeper of this skull
Made elemental, historic, parentless by our
Sailor boy who thinks of home, voyages laden, will
Not say, "Alas! I did not know him at all."

KENNETH PATCHEN
(1911–1972)

I DON'T WANT TO STARTLE YOU
but they are going to kill most of us

I knew the General only by name of course.
I said Wartface what have you done with her?
I said you dirty louse tell me where she is now?
His duck-eyes shifted to the Guard. All right, Sam.
I saw a photograph of the old prick's wife on the desk;
Face smiling like a bag of money on a beggar's grave.
Who is that fat turd I said—he hit me with his jewelled fist.
While his man held me he put a lighted cigarette on my eyelid.
I smelt the burning flesh through his excellent perfume.
On the wall it said *Democracy must be saved at all costs.*
The floor was littered with letters of endorsement from liberals
And intellectuals: "your high ideals," "liberty," "human justice."
Stalin's picture spotted between Hoover's and a group-shot of
    the DAR.
I brought my knee up suddenly and caught him in the nuts.
A little foam trickled from his flabby puss. All right, Sam.
They led me into a yard and through a city of iron cells.
I saw all the boys: Lenin, Trotsky, Nin, Pierce, Rosa Luxemburg. . .
Their eyes were confident, beautiful, unafraid . . .
We came finally to an immense hall protected by barbed wire
And machine guns: Hitler, Benny Mussolini, Roosevelt, and all
The big and little wigs were at table, F.D.'s arm around Adolf,
Chiang Kai-shek's around the Pope, all laughing fit to kill.
As soon as a treaty was signed, out the window it went;
But how they fumbled at each other under the table!
I snatched up a menu:
        Grilled Japanese Soldier on Toast
        Fried Revolutionaries à la Dirty Joe
        Roast Worker Free Style

Hamstrung Colonial Stew, British Special
Gassed Child's Breast, International Favorite
Wine list—Blood 1914, '15, '17, '23, '34, '36, '40, etc.
So much fresh meat I thought! A butchers' holiday . . .
The General paused to enjoy the floorshow:
On a raised platform little groups of people stood.
Flags told their nationality; orators told them what to do.
As the bands blared they rushed at each other with bayonets.
The dead and dying were dragged off and others brought on.
Sweat streamed from the orators; the musicians wobbled crazily.
The Big Shots were mad with joy, juggling in their seats like
    monkeys.
And they never get wise the General said as we moved on.
Out in the air again . . .
A line of petty officials and war-pimps waited before the door.
As we approached they drew aside respectfully to let the General in.
I heard a woman moaning and I knew what they wanted there.
Now do you know what we've done with her the General said.
To go mad or to die . . .
They forced me to watch as the General went up to her and
Her eyes were looking at me.

WILLIAM EVERSON
(1912-)

The Raid

They came out of the sun undetected,
Who had lain in the thin ships
All night long on the cold ocean,
Watched Vega down, the Wain hover,
Drank in the weakening dawn their brew,
And sent the lumbering death-laden birds
Level along the decks.

They came out of the sun with their guns geared,
Saw the soft and easy shape of that island
Laid on the sea,
An unwakening woman,
Its deep hollows and its flowing folds
Veiled in the garlands of its morning mists.
Each of them held in his aching eyes the erotic image,
And then tipped down,
In the target's trance,
In the ageless instant of the long descent,
And saw sweet chaos blossom below,
And felt in that flower the years release.

The perfect achievement.
They went back toward the sun crazy with joy,
Like wild birds weaving,
Drunkenly stunting;
Passed out over edge of that injured island,
Sought the rendezvous on the open sea
Where the ships would be waiting.

None were there.
Neither smoke nor smudge;

Neither spar nor splice nor rolling raft.
Only the wide waiting waste,
That each of them saw with intenser sight
Than he ever had spared it,
Who circled that spot,
The spent gauge caught in its final flutter,
And straggled down on their wavering wings
From the vast sky,
From the endless spaces,
Down at last for the low hover,
And the short quick quench of the sea.

MAY SARTON
(*1912–*)

Navigator

This lazy prince of tennis balls and lutes,
Marvelous redhead who could eat and have his cake,
Collector of hot jazz, Japanese prints, rare books,
The charming winner who takes all for the game's sake,
Is now disciplined, changed, and wrung into a man.
For war's sake, in six months, this can be done.

Now he is groomed and cared for like a fighting cock,
His blood enriched, his athlete's nerve refined
In crucibles of tension to be electric under shock,
His intellect composed for action and designed
To map a bomber's passage to Berlin by stars,
Precision's instrument that neither doubts nor fears.

This can be done in six months. Take a marvelous boy
And knead him into manhood for destruction's joy.
This can be done in six months, but we never tried
Until we needed the lute player's sweet lifeblood.
O the composed mind and the electric nerve
Were never trained like this to build, to love, to serve.

Look at him now and swear by every bomb he will release,
This shall be done. This shall be better done in peace!

KARL SHAPIRO

(1913–)

Troop Train

It stops the town we come through. Workers raise
Their oily arms in good salute and grin.
Kids scream as at a circus. Business men
Glance hopefully and go their measured way.
And women standing at their dumbstruck door
More slowly wave and seem to warn us back,
As if a tear blinding the course of war
Might once dissolve our iron in their sweet wish.

Fruit of the world, O clustered on ourselves
We hang as from a cornucopia
In total friendliness, with faces bunched
To spray the streets with catcalls and with leers.
A bottle smashes on the moving ties
And eyes fixed on a lady smiling pink
Stretch like a rubber-band and snap and sting
The mouth that wants the drink-of-water kiss.

And on through crummy continents and days,
Deliberate, grimy, slightly drunk we crawl,
The good-bad boys of circumstance and chance,
Whose bucket-helmets bang the empty wall
Where twist the murdered bodies of our packs
Next to the guns that only seem themselves.
And distance like a strap adjusted shrinks,
Tighten across the shoulder and holds firm.

Here is a deck of cards; out of this hand
Dealer, deal me my luck, a pair of bulls,
The right draw to a flush, the one-eyed jack.
Diamonds and hearts are red but spades are black,

And spades are spades and clubs are clovers—black.
But deal me winners, souvenirs of peace.
This stands to reason and arithmetic,
Luck also travels and not all come back.

Trains lead to ships and ships to death or trains,
And trains to death or trucks, and trucks to death,
Or trucks lead to the march, the march to death,
Or that survival which is all our hope;
And death leads back to trucks and trains and ships,
But life leads to the march, O flag! at last
The place of life found after trains and death—
Nightfall of nations brilliant after war.

Elegy for a Dead Soldier

I

A white sheet on the tail-gate of a truck
Becomes an altar; two small candlesticks
Sputter at each side of the crucifix
Laid round with flowers brighter than the blood,
Red as the red of our apocalypse,
Hibiscus that a marching man will pluck
To stick into his rifle or his hat,
And great blue morning-glories pale as lips
That shall no longer taste or kiss or swear.
The wind begins a low magnificat,
The chaplain chats, the palmtrees swirl their hair,
The columns come together through the mud.

II

We too are ashes as we watch and hear
The psalm, the sorrow, and the simple praise
Of one whose promised thoughts of other days
Were such as ours, but now wholly destroyed,
The service record of his youth wiped out,
His dream dispersed by shot, must disappear.
What can we feel but wonder at a loss
That seems to point at nothing but the doubt
Which flirts our sense of luck into the ditch?
Reader of Paul who prays beside this fosse,
Shall we believe our eyes or legends rich
With glory and rebirth beyond the void?

III

For this comrade is dead, dead in the war,
A young man out of millions yet to live,

One cut away from all that war can give,
Freedom of self and peace to wander free.
Who mourns in all this sober multitude
Who did not feel the bite of it before
The bullet found its aim? This worthy flesh,
This boy laid in a coffin and reviewed—
Who has not wrapped himself in this same flag,
Heard the light fall of dirt, his wound still fresh,
Felt his eyes closed, and heard the distant brag
Of the last volley of humanity?

IV

By chance I saw him die, stretched on the ground,
A tattooed arm lifted to take the blood
Of someone else sealed in a tin. I stood
During the last delirium that stays
The intelligence a tiny moment more,
And then the strangulation, the last sound.
The end was sudden, like a foolish play,
A stupid fool slamming a foolish door,
The absurd catastrophe, half-prearranged,
And all the decisive things still left to say.
So we disbanded, angrier and unchanged,
Sick with the utter silence of dispraise.

V

We ask for no statistics of the killed,
For nothing political impinges on
This single casualty, or all those gone,
Missing or healing, sinking or dispersed,
Hundreds of thousands counted, millions lost.
More than an accident and less than willed
Is every fall, and this one like the rest.
However others calculate the cost,
To us the final aggregate is *one,*
One with a name, one transferred to the blest;
And though another stoops and takes the gun,
We cannot add the second to the first.

VI

I would not speak for him who could not speak
Unless my fear were true: he was not wronged,
He knew to which decision he belonged
But let it choose itself. Ripe in instinct,
Neither the victim nor the volunteer,
He followed, and the leaders could not seek
Beyond the followers. Much of this he knew;
The journey was a detour that would steer
Into the Lincoln Highway of a land
Remorselessly improved, excited, new,
And that was what he wanted. He had planned
To earn and drive. He and the world had winked.

VII

No history deceived him, for he knew
Little of times and armies not his own;
He never felt that peace was but a loan,
Had never questioned the idea of gain.
Beyond the headlines once or twice he saw
The gathering of a power by the few
But could not tell their names; he cast his vote,
Distrusting all the elected but not law.
He laughed at socialism; *on mourrait*
Pour les industriels? He shed his coat
And not for brotherhood, but for his pay.
To him the red flag marked the sewer main.

VIII

Above all else he loathed the homily,
The slogan and the ad. He paid his bill,
But not for Congressmen at Bunker Hill.
Ideals were few and those there were not made
For conversation. He belonged to church
But never spoke of God. The Christmas tree,
The Easter egg, baptism, he observed,
Never denied the preacher on his perch,

And would not sign Resolved That or Whereas.
Softness he had and hours and nights reserved
For thinking, dressing, dancing to the jazz.
His laugh was real, his manners were homemade.

IX

Of all men poverty pursued him least;
He was ashamed of all the down and out,
Spurned the panhandler like an uneasy doubt,
And saw the unemployed as a vague mass
Incapable of hunger or revolt.
He hated other races, south or east,
And shoved them to the margin of his mind.
He could recall the justice of the Colt,
Take interest in a gang-war like a game.
His ancestry was somewhere far behind
And left him only his peculiar name.
Doors opened, and he recognized no class.

X

His children would have known a heritage,
Just or unjust, the richest in the world,
The quantum of all art and science curled
In the horn of plenty, bursting from the horn,
A people bathed in honey, Paris come,
Vienna transferred with the highest wage,
A World's Fair spread to Phoenix, Jacksonville,
Earth's capital, the new Byzantium,
Kingdom of man—who knows? Hollow or firm,
No man can ever prophesy until
Out of our death some undiscovered germ,
Whole toleration or pure peace is born.

XI

The time to mourn is short that best becomes
The military dead. We lift and fold the flag,

Lay bare the coffin with its written tag,
And march away. Behind, four others wait
To lift the box, the heaviest of loads.
The anesthetic afternoon benumbs,
Sickens our senses, forces back our talk.
We know that others on tomorrow's roads
Will fall, ourselves perhaps, the man beside,
Over the world the threatened, all who walk:
And could we mark the grave of him who died
We would write this beneath his name and date:

EPITAPH

Underneath this wooden cross there lies
A Christian killed in battle. You who read,
Remember that this stranger died in pain;
And passing here, if you can lift your eyes
Upon a peace kept by a human creed,
Know that one soldier has not died in vain.

Fox Hole

Quintana lay in the shallow grave of coral. The guns boomed stupidly fifty yards away. The plasma trickled into his arm. Naked and filthy, covered with mosquitoes, he looked at me as I read his white cloth tag. How do you feel, Quintana? He looks away from my gaze. I lie: we'll get you out of here sometime today.

I never saw him again, dead or alive. Skin and bones, with eyes as soft as soot, neck long as a thigh, a cross on his breastbone not far from the dog tags. El Greco was all I could think of. Quintana lying in his shallow foxhole waiting to be evacuated. A dying man with a Spanish name equals El Greco. A truck driver from Dallas probably.

When the Japs were making the banzai charge, to add insult to death, they came at us screaming the supreme insult: *Babe Ruth, go to hell!* The Americans, on the other hand, when the Japs flew over dropping sticks of explosives, shouted into the air, as if they could hear: *Tojo, eat shit!*

Soldiers fall in love with the enemy all too easily. It's the allies they hate. Every war is its own excuse. That's why they're all surrounded with ideals. That's why they're all crusades.

Homecoming

Lost in the vastness of the void Pacific
My thousand days of exile, pain,
Bid me farewell. Gone is the Southern Cross
To her own sky, fallen a continent
Under the wave, dissolved the bitterest isles
In their salt element,
And here upon the deck the mist encloses
My smile that would light up all darkness
And ask forgiveness of the things that thrust
Shame and all death on millions and on me.

We bring no raw materials from the East
But green-skinned men in blue-lit holds
And lunatics impounded between-decks;
The mighty ghoul-ship that we ride exhales
The sickly-sweet stench of humiliation,
And even the majority, untouched by steel
Or psychoneurosis, stare with eyes in rut,
Their hands a rabble to snatch the riches
Of glittering shops and girls.

Because I am angry at this kindness which
Is both habitual and contradictory
To the life of armies, now I stand alone
And hate the swarms of khaki men that crawl
Like lice upon the wrinkled hide of earth,
Infesting ships as well. Not otherwise
Could I lean outward piercing fog to find
Our sacred bridge of exile and return.
My tears are psychological, not poems
To the United States; my smile is prayer.

Gnawing the thin slops of anxiety,
Escorted by the groundswell and by gulls,
In silence and with mystery we enter
The territorial waters. Not till then
Does that convulsive terrible joy, more sudden

And brilliant than the explosion of a ship,
Shatter the tensions of the heaven and sea
To crush a hundred thousand skulls
And liberate in that high burst of love
The imprisoned souls of soldiers and of me.

After the War

After a war the boys play soldier with real weapons. This is a real hand grenade, a pineapple. The killing stuff has been removed but the pin remains to pull out and push in. There is a clip to hang it from your belt. The pineapple is a red-brown iron the color of—a pineapple, very heavy to hold, very heavy to throw, though small. All the boys own a pineapple. The squares are cut deep in the metal fruit. When it explodes, we say, you have diced pineapple and dying men and a hole in the ground.

The dummy rifles are dark-brown wood. Every part is round and smooth. There is no metal, no trigger assembly. The dummy muzzle comes to a rubber end like a truncheon or a heavy walking stick. It is five feet tall and too heavy for boys to hold out straight in the standing position, but fine to hold prone or stand in the corner of the bedroom.

The shallow helmet is rough to the feel, a greenish basin with a cocky steel brim. Inside, the webbing is leather to fit the skull and carry the shock. Mine has a handsome dent in the top, a round dent with a crease at the bottom. There is a delicate line of rust in the crease, a close call for somebody.

Today we play on the gray wooden battleship built on the grass for the sailors' drills. This must be the biggest toy in the world, a full-sized ship, a ship out of water, all above ground, without a keel. The Naval Base is always open to boys. The Naval Base is filled with flowered walks and neat straight lines and white-washed curbs. The officers' houses are white and face the Bay. The wooden battleship is a school. It never rocks but runs up fluttering flags. The ship browses at peace among the flowers of the Naval Base. The Shore Police in their sentry boxes at the main entrance don't even notice us as we come and go. We are part of the game.

The shell-shocked newsman stomps down Granby Street, shouting commands and thumping his truncheon-stick on the ground.

Nobody laughs at him; everyone says he is harmless. The fits
of stomping and shouting commands come once or twice a
day. Then he subsides in a truce with himself. When there are
parades he stands at attention.

Leaving the troopship, men hacked at walls, slit mattresses, broke
pipes, gouged at lounge-room ornamentation, middle-class
British taste for luxury liners, made minor desecrations of the
great gray leviathan. On this voyage of forty days and forty
nights the Americans consumed a quarter of a million Coca-
Colas, the sergeant says, and spits between his feet.

The General returns with the power of a god. His disgrace is a
triumph. The world pours at his feet like a tide; it swirls
through cities and engulfs skyscrapers. Men become fright-
ened at their own frenzy. In Chicago the cheering and weep-
ing are endemic, maniacal. The General is handsome, arro-
gant, and wrong. Such a General might be the President. He
leaves his car to lay a wreath on a bridge across the poisonous
Chicago River. He delivers his profile to rich and poor. In the
war his communiqués always mentioned God. We hated him.

Human Nature

For months and years in a forgotten war
I rode the battle-gray Diesel-stinking ships
Among the brilliantly advertised Pacific Islands,
Coasting the sinister New Guinea Coasts,
All during the killing and hating of a forgotten war.
Now when I drive behind a Diesel-stinking bus
On the way to the university to teach
Stevens and Pound and Mallarmé,
I am homesick for war.

57

ROBERT HAYDEN

(1913–1980)

Belsen, Day of Liberation

(for Rosey)

Her parents and her dolls destroyed,
    her childhood foreclosed,
she watched the foreign soldiers from
    the sunlit window whose black bars

Were crooked crosses inked upon
    her pallid face. "Liebchen,
Liebchen, you should be in bed."
    But she felt ill no longer.

And because that day was a holy day
    when even the dead, it seemed,
must rise, she was allowed to stay
    and see the golden strangers who

Were Father, Brother, and her dream
    of God. Afterwards
she said, "They were so beautiful,
    and they were not afraid."

RANDALL JARRELL
(1914–1965)

Eighth Air Force

If, in an odd angle of the hutment,
A puppy laps the water from a can
Of flowers, and the drunk sergeant shaving
Whistles O Paradiso!—shall I say that man
Is not as men have said: a wolf to man?

The other murderers troop in yawning;
Three of them play Pitch, one sleeps, and one
Lies counting missions, lies there sweating
Till even his heart beats: One; One; One.
O murderers! . . . Still, this is how it's done:

This is a war. . . . But since these play, before they die,
Like puppies with their puppy; since, a man,
I did as these have done, but did not die—
I will content the people as I can
And give up these to them: Behold the man!

I have suffered, in a dream, because of him,
Many things; for this last saviour, man,
I have lied as I lie now. But what is lying?
Men wash their hands, in blood, as best they can:
I find no fault in this just man.

A Front

Fog over the base: the beams ranging
From the five towers pull home from the night
The crews cold in fur, the bombers banging
Like lost trucks down the levels of the ice.
A glow drifts in like mist (how many tons of it?),
Bounces to a roll, turns suddenly to steel
And tires and turrets, huge in the trembling light.
The next is high, and pulls up with a wail,
Comes round again—no use. And no use for the rest
In drifting circles out along the range;
Holding no longer, changed to a kinder course,
The flights drone southward through the steady rain.
The base is closed. . . . But one voice keeps on calling,
The lowering pattern of the engines grows;
The roar gropes downward in its shaky orbit
For the lives the season quenches. Here below
They beg, order, are not heard; and hear the darker
Voice rising: *Can't you hear me? Over. Over*—
All the air quivers, and the east sky glows.

The Death of the Ball Turret Gunner

From my mother's sleep I fell into the State,
And I hunched in its belly till my wet fur froze.
Six miles from earth, loosed from its dream of life,
I woke to black flak and the nightmare fighters.
When I died they washed me out of the turret with a hose.

Mail Call

The letters always just evade the hand.
One skates like a stone into a beam, falls like a bird.
Surely the past from which the letters rise
Is waiting in the future, past the graves?
The soldiers are all haunted by their lives.

Their claims upon their kind are paid in paper
That establishes a presence, like a smell.
In letters and in dreams they see the world.
They are waiting: and the years contract
To an empty hand, to one unuttered sound—

The soldier simply wishes for his name.

A War

There set out, slowly, for a Different World,
At four, on winter mornings, different legs . . .
You can't break eggs without making an omelette
—That's what they tell the eggs.

The Range in the Desert

Where the lizard ran to its little prey
And a man on a horse rode by in a day
They set their hangars: a continent
Taught its conscripts its unloved intent
In the scrawled fire, the singing lead—
Protocols of the quick and dead.
The wounded gunner, his missions done,
Fired absently in the range's sun;
And, chained with cartridges, the clerk
Sat sweating at his war-time work.
The cold flights bombed—again, again—
The craters of the lunar plain. . . .

All this was priceless: men were paid
For these rehearsals of the raids
That used up cities at a rate
That left the coals without a State
To call another's; till the worse
Ceded at last, without remorse,
Their conquests to their conquerors.
The equations were without two powers.

Profits and death grow marginal:
Only the mourning and the mourned recall
The wars we lose, the wars we win;
And the world is—what it has been.

The lizard's tongue licks angrily
The shattered membranes of the fly.

The Lines

After the centers' naked files, the basic line
Standing outside a building in the cold
Of the late or early darkness, waiting
For meals or mail or salvage, or to wait
To form a line to form a line to form a line;
After the things have learned that they are things,
Used up as things are, pieces of the plain
Flat object-language of a child or states;
After the lines, through trucks, through transports, to the lines
Where the things die as though they were not things—
But lie as numbers in the crosses' lines;
After the files that ebb into the rows
Of the white beds of the quiet wards, the lines
Where some are salvaged for their state, but some
Remanded, useless, to the centers' files;
After the naked things, told they are men,
Have lined once more for papers, pensions—suddenly
The lines break up, for good; and for a breath,
The longest of their lives, the men are free.

A Field Hospital

He stirs, beginning to awake.
A kind of ache
Of knowing troubles his blind warmth; he moans,
And the high hammering drone
Of the first crossing fighters shakes
His sleep to pieces, rakes
The darkness with its skidding bursts, is done.
All that he has known

Floods in upon him; but he dreads
The crooked thread
Of fire upon the darkness: "The great drake
Flutters to the icy lake—
The shotguns stammer in my head.
I lie in my own bed,"
He whispers, "dreaming"; and he thinks to wake.
The old mistake.

A cot creaks; and he hears the groan
He thinks his own—
And groans, and turns his stitched, blind, bandaged head
Up to the tent-flap, red
With dawn. A voice says, "Yes, this one";
His arm stings; then, alone,
He neither knows, remembers—but instead
Sleeps, comforted.

WELDON KEES
(1914–1955)

June 1940

"Yet these elegies are to this generation in no sense consolatory.
They may be to the next. All a poet can do today is warn."
"The old Lie: Dulce et decorum est
Pro patria mori."

—WILFRED OWEN

It is summer, and treachery blurs with the sounds of midnight,
The lights blink off at the closing of a door,
And I am alone in a worn-out town in wartime,
Thinking of those who were trapped by hysteria once before.

Flaubert and Henry James and Owen,
Bourne with his crooked back, Rilke and Lawrence, Joyce—
Gun-shy, annoyers, sick of the kill, the watchers,
Suffered the same attack till it broke them or left its scars.

Now the heroes of March are the sorriest fools of April:
The beaters of drums, the flag-kissing men, whose eyes
Once saw the murder, are washing it clean, accusing:
"You are the cowards! All that we told you before was lies!"

It is summer again, the evening is warm and silent.
The windows are dark and the mountains are miles away.
And the men who were haters of war are mounting the platforms.
An idiot wind is blowing; the conscience dies.

JOHN BERRYMAN
(1914–1972)

The Moon and the Night and the Men

On the night of the Belgian surrender the moon rose
Late, a delayed moon, and a violent moon
For the English or the American beholder;
The French beholder. It was a cold night,
People put on their wraps, the troops were cold
No doubt, despite the calendar, no doubt
Numbers of refugees coughed, and the sight
Or sound of some killed others. A cold night.

On Outer Drive there was an accident:
A stupid well-intentioned man turned sharp
Right and abruptly he became an angel
Fingering an unfamiliar harp,
Or screamed in hell, or was nothing at all.
Do not imagine this is unimportant.
He was a part of the night, part of the land,
Part of the bitter and exhausted ground
Out of which memory grows.

                              Michael and I
Stared at each other over chess, and spoke
As little as possible, and drank and played.
The chessmen caught in the European eye,
Neither of us I think had a free look
Although the game was fair. The move one made
It was difficult at last to keep one's mind on.
'Hurt and unhappy' said the man in London.
We said to each other. The time is coming near
When none shall have books or music, none his dear,
And only a fool will speak aloud his mind.

66

History is approaching a speechless end,
As Henry Adams said. Adams was right.

All this occurred on the night when Leopold
Fulfilled the treachery four years before
Begun—or was he well-intentioned, more
Roadmaker to hell than king? At any rate,
The moon came up late and the night was cold,
Many men died—although we know the fate
Of none, nor of anyone, and the war
Goes on, and the moon in the breast of man is cold.

PETER VIERECK
(1916–)

Vale from Carthage

(*for my brother, 1944*)

I, now at Carthage. He, shot dead at Rome.
Shipmates last May. "And what if one of us,"
I asked last May, in fun, in gentleness,
"Wears doom, like dungarees, and doesn't know?"
He laughed, "*Not see Times Square again?*" The foam,
Feathering across that deck a year ago,
Swept those five words—like seeds—beyond the seas
    Into his future. There they grew like trees;
    And as he passed them there next spring, they laid
    Upon his road of fire their sudden shade.
Though he had always scraped his mess-kit pure
And scrubbed redeemingly his barracks floor,
Though all his buttons glowed their ritual-hymn
Like cloudless moons to intercede for him,
No furlough fluttered from the sky. He will
Not see Times Square—he will not see—he will
Not see Times
          change; at Carthage (while my friend,
Living those words at Rome, screamed in the end)
I saw an ancient Roman's tomb and read
"*Vale*" in stone. Here two wars mix their dead:

Author's Note: The word "vale" (Latin for "farewell") was used on Roman tombstones. "Ave atque vale" is, of course, the phrase immortalized by Catullus in his elegy to his brother, killed fighting for Rome in an older war than mine. As a sergeant in the U.S. Army's African campaign in March 1944, I was among the Roman tombstones in the ruins of Carthage when I heard the news that my brother was killed by a German bullet in the Anzio beachhead, near Rome. He and I had met last at Times Square, New York.

Roman, my shipmate's dream walks hand in hand
With yours tonight ("New York again" and "Rome"),
Like widowed sisters bearing water home
On tired heads through hot Tunisian sand
In good cool urns, and says, "I understand."
Roman, you'll see your Forum Square no more;
What's left but this to say of any war?

Kilroy

(for John H. Finley, Jr.)

1.

Also Ulysses once—that other war.
　　(Is it because we find his scrawl
　　Today on every privy door
　　That we forget his ancient rôle?)
Also was there—he did it for the wages—
When a Cathay-drunk Genoese set sail.
Whenever "longen folk to goon on pilgrimages,"
Kilroy is there;
　　　　　　he tells The Miller's Tale.

2.

At times he seems a paranoiac king
Who stamps his crest on walls and says, "My own!"
But in the end he fades like a lost tune,
Tossed here and there, whom all the breezes sing.
"Kilroy was here"; these words sound wanly gay,
　　　　Haughty yet tired with long marching.
He is Orestes—guilty of what crime?—
　　　　For whom the Furies still are searching;
　　　　When they arrive, they find their prey
(Leaving his name to mock them) went away.
Sometimes he does not flee from them in time:
"Kilroy was—"
　　　　　　(with his blood a dying man
　　　　Wrote half the phrase out in Bataan.)

Editor's note: An example of an unfaked epic spirit emerging from the war was the expression "Kilroy was here," scribbled everywhere by American soldiers and implying that nothing was too adventurous or remote.

3.

Kilroy, beware. "HOME" is the final trap
That lurks for you in many a wily shape:
In pipe-and-slippers plus a Loyal Hound
    Or fooling around, just fooling around.
Kind to the old (their warm Penelope)
But fierce to boys,
            thus "home" becomes that sea,
Horribly disguised, where you were always drowned,—
    (How could suburban Crete condone
The yarns you would have V-mailed from the sun?)—
And folksy fishes sip Icarian tea.
One stab of hopeless wings imprinted your
    Exultant Kilroy-signature
Upon sheer sky for all the world to stare:
        "I was there! I was there! I was there!"

4.

God is like Kilroy; He, too, sees it all;
That's how He knows of every sparrow's fall;
That's why we prayed each time the tightropes cracked
On which our loveliest clowns contrived their act.
The G. I. Faustus who was
               everywhere
Strolled home again. "What was it like outside?"
Asked Can't, with his good neighbors Ought and But
And pale Perhaps and grave-eyed Better Not;
For "Kilroy" means: the world is very wide.
    He was there, he was there, he was there!

And in the suburbs Can't sat down and cried.

Ripeness Is All

Through nights of slanting rain
Marchers are planting pain;
Gardeners in boots
Plant tender seeds of mines
Where the dimmed flashlight shines,
Nursing the wire-vines,
Hiding the roots.

Boys in green raincoats scamper
Where grass will soon be damper
When ripeness murders.
How fast the seeds grow high!
Blossoming, towards the sky
Pain's gaudy petals fly,
White with red borders.

JOHN CIARDI

(1916–1986)

Return

Once more the searchlights beckon from the night
The homing drone of bombers. One by one
They strike like neon down the plastic dome
Of darkness palaced on our sea and sight
Where avenues of light flower on a stone
To bring the theorem and its thunder home.

Wheels touch and snub, and on the wing's decline
From air and motion into mass and weight
Grace falls from metal like a dancer's glove
Dropped from the hand. She pauses for the sign
Of one more colored light, and home and late
Crosses to darkness like an end of love.

Under the celebration of the sky
Still calling home the living to their pause
The hatches spill the lucky and returned
Onto the solid stone of not-to-die
And see their eyes are lenses and they house
Reel after reel of how a city burned.

Elegy for a Cove Full of Bones

—Saipan
Dec. 16, '44

Tibia, tarsal, skull, and shin:
Bones come out where the guns go in.
Hermit crabs like fleas in armor
Crawl the coral-pock, a tremor
Moves the sea, and surf falls cold
On coves where glutton rats grow bold.
In the brine of sea and weather
Shredded flesh transforms to leather,
And the wind and sea invade
The rock-smudge that the flame throwers made.

Death is lastly a debris
Folding on the folding sea:
Blankets, boxes, belts, and bones,
And a jelly on the stones.
What the body taught the mind
Flies explore and do not find.
Here the certain stood to die
Passionately to prove a lie.
At the end a covenant's pall
Of stones made solid, palpable,
Moves the victory to the sea,
And the wind indifferently.

Hate is nothing, pity less.
Angers lead us to digress:
I shall murder if I can.
Spill the jellies of a man.
Or be luckless and be spilled
In the wreck of those killed.

Nothing modifies our end:
Nothing in the ruin will mend.

If I moralize, forgive:
Error is the day we live.
In the ammoniac coves of death
I am choked for living breath.
I am tired of thinking guns,
Knowing where the bullet runs.
I am dreaming of a kiss
And a flesh more whole than this.
I am pondering a root
To destroy the cove-rat's loot.
I am measuring a place
For the living's living grace.
I am running from the breath
Of the vaporing coves of death.
I have seen our failure in
Tibia, tarsal, skull, and shin.

Elegy Just in Case

Here lie Ciardi's pearly bones
In their ripe organic mess.
Jungle blown, his chromosomes
Breed to a new address.

Was it bullets or a wind
Or a rip cord fouled on chance?
Artifacts the natives find
Decorate them when they dance.

Here lies the sgt.'s mortal wreck
Lily spiked and termite kissed,
Spiders pendant from his neck
And a beetle on his wrist.

Bring the tick and southern flies
Where the land crabs run unmourning
Through a night of jungle skies
To a climeless morning.

And bring the chalked eraser here
Fresh from rubbing out his name.
Burn the crew-board for a bier.
(Also Colonel what's-his-name.)

Let no dice be stored and still.
Let no poker deck be torn.
But pour the smuggled rye until
The barracks threshold is outworn.

File the papers, pack the clothes,
Send the coded word through air—
"We regret and no one knows
Where the sgt. goes from here."

"Missing as of inst. oblige,
Deepest sorrow and remain—"
Shall I grin at persiflage?
Could I have my skin again

Would I choose a business form
Stilted mute as a giraffe,
Or a pinstripe unicorn
On a cashier's epitaph?

Darling, darling, just in case
Rivets fail or engines burn,
I forget the time and place
But your flesh was sweet to learn.

Swift and single as a shark
I have seen you churn my sleep
Now if beetles hunt my dark
What will beetles find to keep?

Fractured meat and open bone—
Nothing single or surprised.
Fragments of a written stone
Undeciphered but surmised.

Sea Burial

Through the sea's crust of prisms looking up
Into the run of light above the swell
And down a fathom, down a fathom more
Until the darkness closes like a shell.

Oblique, like fall of leaves down the wet glide
Of season and surrender from the tree
Of life across the windows of a wind
To the final ruined lawn beneath a sea.

Glide, glide and fall. How lightly death goes down
Into the crushing fog, pale and refracted.
Seen dimly and then lost, like jellyfish
Flowering a tide, expanded, then contracted,

One more expanded, and then closed forever
To make a stain on stone and liquefy
The memory that kissed a mountain girl
And ran on grass as if it could not die.

On a Photo of Sgt. Ciardi a Year Later

The sgt. stands so fluently in leather,
So poster-holstered and so newsreel-jawed
As death's costumed and fashionable brother,
My civil memory is overawed.

Behind him see the circuses of doom
Dance a finale chorus on the sun.
He leans on gun sights, doesn't give a damn
For dice or stripes, and waits to see the fun.

The cameraman whose ornate public eye
Invented that fine bravura look of calm
At murderous clocks hung ticking in the sky
Palmed the deception off without a qualm.

Even the camera, focused and exact
To a two dimensional conclusion,
Uttered its formula of physical fact
Only to lend data to illusion.

The camera always lies. By a law of perception
The obvious surface is always an optical ruse.
The leather was living tissue in its own dimension,
The holsters held benzedrine tablets, the guns were no use.

The careful slouch and dangling cigarette
Were always superstitious as Amen.
The shadow under the shadow is never caught:
The camera photographs the cameraman.

A Box Comes Home

I remember the United States of America
As a flag-draped box with Arthur in it
And six marines to bear it on their shoulders.

I wonder how someone once came to remember
The Empire of the East and the Empire of the West.
As an urn maybe delivered by chariot.

You could bring Germany back on a shield once
And France in a plume. England, I suppose,
Kept coming back a long time as a letter.

Once I saw Arthur dressed as the United States
Of America. Now I see the United States
Of America as Arthur in a flag-sealed domino.

And I would pray more good of Arthur
Than I can wholly believe. I would pray
An agreement with the United States of America

To equal Arthur's living as it equals his dying
At the red-taped grave in Woodmere
By the rain and oakleaves on the domino.

Visibility Zero

All day with mist against the hurdling wind
The lights hung dressed in halves and a blur.
Air that was solid on a hurtling wing
Hangs sodden, and the parked planes wear like fur
Their look of waiting in the liquid pause
Of cloud descended, in a veil of gauze
The three complete and only trees incite
Their separate loss into the early night

Fixed to the gauge that swears we cannot see,
Our engines, blind as junk, await the light.
Cards, dice, and spinning coins turn noisily
Into the separate corners of the night.
This was the day we saw our lives made safe,
The day no engines burned and no one gave
A morning thought to chance, but late in bed
Praised the tiered fog that nowhere touched the dead.

Complete in pause, we woke into no need,
Turned back to sleep, stayed dry, and wished for mail.
Ate, and addressed a holiday—a nod
To cancelled schedules, and a word to tell
Our postponed fear that it was not our choice.
And then, released, the barracks lounging voice
In praise of hours where instruments agree
We need not waken and we need not see.

V-J Day

On the tallest day in time the dead came back.
Clouds met us in the pastures past a world.
By short wave the releases of a rack
Exploded on the interphone's new word.

Halfway past Iwo we jettisoned to sea
Our gift of bombs like tears and tears like bombs
To spring a frolic fountain daintily
Out of the blue metallic seas of doom.

No fire-shot cloud pursued us going home.
No cities cringed and wallowed in the flame.
Far out to sea a blank millennium
Changed us alive, and left us still the same.

Lightened, we banked like jays, antennae squawking.
The four wild metal halos of our props
Blurred into time. The interphone was talking
Abracadabra to the cumulus tops:

Dreamboat three-one to Yearsend—loud and clear,
Angels one-two, on course at one-six-nine.
Magellan to Balboa. Propwash to Century.
How do you read me? Bombay to Valentine.

Fading and out. And all the dead were homing.
(*Wisecrack to Halfmast. Doom to Memory.*)
On the tallest day in time we saw them coming,
Wheels jammed and flaming on a metal sea.

ROBERT LOWELL

(1917–1978)

Memories of West Street and Lepke

Only teaching on Tuesdays, book-worming
in pajamas fresh from the washer each morning,
I hog a whole house on Boston's
"hardly passionate Marlborough Street,"
where even the man
scavenging filth in the back alley trash cans,
has two children, a beach wagon, a helpmate,
and is a "young Republican."
I have a nine months' daughter,
young enough to be my granddaughter.
Like the sun she rises in her flame-flamingo infants' wear.

These are the tranquillized *Fifties*,
and I am forty. Ought I to regret my seedtime?
I was a fire-breathing Catholic C. O.,
and made my manic statement,
telling off the state and president, and then
sat waiting sentence in the bull pen
beside a Negro boy with curlicues
of marijuana in his hair.

Given a year,
I walked on the roof of the West Street Jail, a short
enclosure like my school soccer court,
and saw the Hudson River once a day
through sooty clothesline entanglements
and bleaching khaki tenements.
Strolling, I yammered metaphysics with Abramowitz,
a jaundice-yellow ("it's really tan")
and fly-weight pacifist,
so vegetarian,

he wore rope shoes and preferred fallen fruit.
He tried to convert Bioff and Brown,
the Hollywood pimps, to his diet.
Hairy, muscular, suburban,
wearing chocolate double-breasted suits,
they blew their tops and beat him black and blue.

I was so out of things, I'd never heard
of the Jehovah's Witnesses.
"Are you a C. O.?" I asked a fellow jailbird.
"No," he answered, "I'm a J.W."
He taught me the "hospital tuck,"
and pointed out the T shirted back
of *Murder Incorporated's* Czar Lepke,
there piling towels on a rack,
or dawdling off to his little segregated cell full
of things forbidden the common man:
a portable radio, a dresser, two toy American
flags tied together with a ribbon of Easter palm.
Flabby, bald, lobotomized,
he drifted in a sheepish calm,
where no agonizing reappraisal
jarred his concentration on the electric chair—
hanging like an oasis in his air
of lost connections. . . .

REED WHITTEMORE
(1919–)

Black Cross

I would like to dispense with certain sorrows,
Having no room for unessentials
Like a German death, and travel light,
A better soldier than I am.
Black cross on new lumber, a medal,
The guttural letters of vital statistics,
A helmet—besides, I never knew this man,
How tall with a great chest and long-muscled thighs,
Digging with sweat on his shoulders, marching,
Loving a dark-haired girl he was.
And where he was born and moved with grace
Through a pretty little pattern to this desert place
Is no concern of mine.

White Cross

Blatz was drafted, act of God and neighbors,
For God and neighbors and The Better Life
As Bangor, Boston, Bethlehem and Boise
Live it. Blatz was drafted in the spring.
By summer he had gone abroad to see
What he could do. By winter he was buried.

Poor Blatz. His absence stirs the sale of bonds
On Linden Road, brings tears and pride and emptiness
To Linden Road, alone to Linden Road.
But in another country, by the road
That stretches east to Kairouan and west
To Kasserine, Tebessa and Thelepte

(Kairouan is a place to buy a rug,
A noon dune scene, a trinket dug in the desert,
Not honor. A Souk, a watering point,
A white and holy city, it buries its dead
On the outskirts, under a few weathered stones.
Those are the stones that line the western hills,

The wise dead, the ready dead, the prayed for,
Beards and wrinkles come to their elephant graves),
But in another country strangers pause,
Observing a special silence before his cross,
Reading his name, poor Blatz, and possibly
Dreaming of heroes.

WILLIAM MEREDITH
(1919–)

Airman's Virtue

(after Herbert)

High plane for whom the winds incline,
   Who own but to your own recall,
There is a flaw in your design
   For you must fall.

High cloud whose proud and angry stuff
   Rose up in heat against earth's thrall,
The nodding law has time enough
   To wait your fall.

High sky, full of high shapes and vapors,
   Against whose vault nothing is tall,
It is written that your torch and tapers
   Headlong shall fall.

Only an outward-aching soul
   Can hold in high disdain these ties
And fixing on a farther pole
   Will sheerly rise.

HOWARD NEMEROV

(1920–)

Redeployment

They say the war is over. But water still
Comes bloody from the taps, and my pet cat
In his disorder vomits worms which crawl
Swiftly away. Maybe they leave the house.
These worms are white, and flecked with the cat's blood.

The war may be over. I know a man
Who keeps a pleasant souvenir, he keeps
A soldier's dead blue eyeballs that he found
Somewhere—hard as chalk, and blue as slate.
He clicks them in his pocket while he talks.

And now there are cockroaches in the house,
They get slightly drunk on DDT,
Are fast, hard, shifty—can be drowned but not
Without you hold them under quite some time.
People say the Mexican kind can fly.

The end of the war. I took it quietly
Enough. I tried to wash the dirt out of
My hair and from under my fingernails,
I dressed in clean white clothes and went to bed.
I heard the dust falling between the walls.

A Memory of the War

Most what I know of war is what I learned
When mine was over and they shipped me home.
I'd been a chauffeur with the RAF
And didn't know the first damn thing about
The American way of doing anything
Till they told me I was Officer of the Day
(at midnight, yet) and gave me a whopping great
Blue automatic and sat me on D Deck
At the top of a ladder leading to a hold
Where a couple hundred enlisted men were sleeping,
And said I was to sit there till relieved.
"But what's this for?" I said about the gun,
And was answered: "If this ship shows any sign
Of going down, you shoot down the first son-
ofabitch sticks his head up through this hatch."
So that is what I did, and how I learned
About the War: I sat there till relieved.

World Lines

A War Story

And *there I was,* is how these things begin,
Doing my final exam, a solo test
Of navigation by dead reckoning;
If you got there and back, you had to pass.

I got there in good shape, a mining town
Far north of nowheresville, and had turned for home
When the cloud closed down and the snow swept in,
Nothing but speeding snow and darkness white,

But I found the spur of a railroad headed south,
The Iron Compass, the Lost Flyer's Friend,
And followed that at a couple of hundred feet
Until it tunneled into the side of a hill,

And there I was. What then? What happened then?
Now who was I to know what happened then,
A kid just out of school the year before?
His buttons and bones are somewhere out there still.

Memorial Day, '86

Night Operations, Coastal Command RAF

Remembering that war, I'd near believe
We didn't need the enemy, with whom
Our dark encounters were confused and few
And quickly done, so many of our lot
Did for themselves in folly and misfortune.

Some hit our own barrage balloons, and some
Tripped over power lines, coming in low;
Some swung on takeoff, others overshot,
And two or three forgot to lower the wheels.

There were those that flew the bearing for the course
And flew away forever; and the happy few
That homed on Venus sinking beyond the sea
In fading certitude. For all the skill,
For all the time of training, you might take
The hundred steps in darkness, not the next.

The War in the Air

For a saving grace, we didn't see our dead,
Who rarely bothered coming home to die
But simply stayed away out there
In the clean war, the war in the air.

Seldom the ghosts came back bearing their tales
Of hitting the earth, the incompressible sea,
But stayed up there in the relative wind,
Shades fading in the mind,

Who had no graves but only epitaphs
Where never so many spoke for never so few:
Per ardua, said the partisans of Mars,
Per aspera, to the stars.

That was the good war, the war we won
As if there were no death, for goodness' sake,
With the help of the losers we left out there
In the air, in the empty air.

The Faith

"There are those for whom war is a vocation. . . .
They are mystic soldiers, devout—and killing is
their calling. What of them?"
    —Kenneth Burke

I knew a couple of these dedicates,
The ones that loved the life and volunteered
For more of it after they'd got home free
And honorably discharged with all the gongs.

A strange pair if they ever were a pair
Save in my thought, they never knew each other
Far as I knew though they behaved the same
In combat, coldly reckless and extreme,

Although not out of it: for one was mild
And modest, but the other cantankerous
And insubordinate, was once torn off a strip
Same day as decorated for the same deed.

One aimed his aircraft at a battle cruiser
(it turned out one of ours) and was blown away;
The other signalled from behind the Frisians
That he and his crew were hit and going down,

His voice as neutral as the evening news
That we would hear on our return to base
That night: "From these and other operations
Seven of our aircraft failed to return."

They were the heroes, we others carried the spears
In the war that in the last place had been won
By the duty-bound, the neither more nor less.
And now I can't remember which was which.

IFF

1.

Hate Hitler? No, I spared him hardly a thought.
But Corporal Irmin, first, and later on
The O.C. (Flying), Wing Commander Briggs,
And the station C. O. Group Captain Ormery—
Now there were men were objects fit to hate,
Hitler a moustache and a little curl
In the middle of his forehead, whereas these
Bastards were bastards in your daily life,
With Power in their pleasure, smile or frown.

2.

Not to forget my navigator Bert,
Who shyly explained to me that the Jews
Were ruining England and Hitler might be wrong
But he had the right idea . . . We were a crew,
And went on so, the one pair left alive
Of a dozen that chose each other flipping coins
At the OTU, but spoke no civil word
Thereafter, beyond the words that had to do
With the drill for going out and getting back.

3.

One night, with a dozen squadrons coming home
To Manston, the tower gave us orbit and height
To wait our turn in their lofty waiting-room,
And on every circuit, when we crossed the Thames,

IFF = Identification Friend or Foe, a signalling device carried on aircraft for that
       purpose
OTU = Operational Training Unit

Our gunners in the estuary below
Loosed off a couple of dozen rounds on spec,
Defending the Commonwealth as detailed to do,
Their lazy lights so slow, then whipping past.
All the above were friends. And then the foe.

A Fable of the War

The full moon is partly hidden by cloud,
The snow that fell when we came off the boat
Has stopped by now, and it is turning colder.
I pace the platform under the blue lights,
Under a frame of glass and emptiness
In a station whose name I do not know.

Suddenly, passing the known and unknown
Bowed faces of my company, the sad
And potent outfit of the armed, I see
That we are dead. By stormless Acheron
We stand easy, and the occasional moon
Strikes terribly from steel and bone alike.

Our flesh, I see, was too corruptible
For the huge work of death. Only the blind
Crater of the eye can suffer well
The midnight cold of stations in no place,
And hold the tears of pity frozen that
They will implacably reflect on war.

But I have read that God let Solomon
Stand upright, although dead, until the temple
Should be raised up, that demons forced to the work
Might not revolt before the thing was done.
And the king stood, until a little worm
Had eaten through the stick he leaned upon.

So, gentlemen—by greatcoat, cartridge belt
And helmet held together for the time—

In honorably enduring here we seek
The second death. Until the worm shall bite
To betray us, lean each man on his gun
That the great work not falter but go on.

RICHARD WILBUR

(1921–)

Tywater

Death of Sir Nihil, book the *nth*,
Upon the charred and clotted sward,
Lacking the lily of our Lord,
Alases of the hyacinth.

Could flicker from behind his ear
A whistling silver throwing knife
And with a holler punch the life
Out of a swallow in the air.

Behind the lariat's butterfly
Shuttled his white and gritted grin,
And cuts of sky would roll within
The noose-hole, when he spun it high.

The violent, neat and practiced skill
Was all he loved and all he learned;
When he was hit, his body turned
To clumsy dirt before it fell.

And what to say of him, God knows.
Such violence. And such repose.

Place Pigalle

Now homing tradesmen scatter through the streets
Toward suppers, thinking on improved conditions,
While evening, with a million simple fissions,
Takes up its warehouse watches, storefront beats,
By nursery windows its assigned positions.

Now at the corners of the Place Pigalle
Bright bars explode against the dark's embraces;
The soldiers come, the boys with ancient faces,
Seeking their ancient friends, who stroll and loll
Amid the glares and glass: electric graces.

The puppies are asleep, and snore the hounds;
But here wry hares, the soldier and the whore,
Mark off their refuge with a gaudy door,
Brazen at bay, and boldly out of bounds:
The puppies dream, the hounds superbly snore.

Ionized innocence: this pair reclines,
She on the table, he in a tilting chair,
With Arden ease; her eyes as pale as air
Travel his priestgoat face; his hand's thick tines
Touch the gold whorls of her Corinthian hair.

"Girl, if I love thee not, then let me die;
Do I not scorn to change my state with kings?
Your muchtouched flesh, incalculable, which wrings
Me so, now shall I gently seize in my
Desperate soldier's hands which kill all things."

First Snow in Alsace

The snow came down last night like moths
Burned on the moon; it fell till dawn,
Covered the town with simple cloths.

Absolute snow lies rumpled on
What shellbursts scattered and deranged,
Entangled railings, crevassed lawn.

As if it did not know they'd changed,
Snow smoothly clasps the roofs of homes
Fear-gutted, trustless and estranged.

The ration stacks are milky domes;
Across the ammunition pile
The snow has climbed in sparkling combs.

You think: beyond the town a mile
Or two, this snowfall fills the eyes
Of soldiers dead a little while.

Persons and persons in disguise,
Walking the new air white and fine,
Trade glances quick with shared surprise.

At children's windows, heaped, benign,
As always, winter shines the most,
And frost makes marvelous designs.

The night guard coming from his post,
Ten first-snows back in thought, walks slow
And warms him with a boyish boast:

He was the first to see the snow.

Mined Country

They have gone into the gray hills quilled with birches,
Drag now their cannon up the chill mountains;
But it's going to be long before
Their war's gone for good.

I tell you it hits at childhood more than churches
Full up with sky or buried town fountains,
Rooms laid open or anything
Cut stone or cut wood,

Seeing the boys come swinging slow over the grass
(Like playing pendulum) their silver plates,
Stepping with care and listening
Hard for hid metal's cry.

It's rightly-called-chaste Belphoebe some would miss,
Some, calendar colts at Kentucky gates;
But the remotest would guess that
Some scheme's gone awry.

Danger is sunk in the pastures, the woods are sly,
Ingenuity's covered with flowers!
We thought woods were wise but never
Implicated, never involved.

Cows in mid-munch go splattered over the sky;
Roses like brush-whores smile from bowers;
Shepherds must learn a new language; this
Isn't going to be quickly solved.

Sunshiny field grass, the woods floor, are so mixed up
With earliest trusts, you have to pick back
Far past all you have learned, to go
Disinherit the dumb child,

Tell him to trust things alike and never to stop
Emptying things, but not let them lack
Love in some manner restored; to be
Sure the whole world's wild.

Anthony Hecht

(1923–)

"More Light! More Light!"

Composed in the Tower before his execution
These moving verses, and being brought at that time
Painfully to the stake, submitted, declaring thus:
"I implore my God to witness that I have made no crime."

Nor was he forsaken of courage, but the death was horrible,
The sack of gunpowder failing to ignite.
His legs were blistered sticks on which the black sap
Bubbled and burst as he howled for the Kindly Light.

And that was but one, and by no means one of the worst;
Permitted at least his pitiful dignity;
And such as were by made prayers in the name of Christ,
That shall judge all men, for his soul's tranquility.

We move now to outside a German wood.
Three men are there commanded to dig a hole
In which the two Jews are ordered to lie down
And be buried alive by the third, who is a Pole.

Not light from the shrine at Weimar beyond the hill
Nor light from heaven appeared. But he did refuse.
A Lüger settled back deeply in its glove.
He was ordered to change places with the Jews.

Much casual death had drained away their souls.
The thick dirt mounted toward the quivering chin.
When only the head was exposed the order came
To dig him out again and to get back in.

No light, no light in the blue Polish eye.
When he finished a riding boot packed down the earth.
The Lüger hovered lightly in its glove.
He was shot in the belly and in three hours bled to death.

No prayers or incense rose up in those hours
Which grew to be years, and every day came mute
Ghosts from the ovens, sifting through crisp air,
And settled upon his eyes in a black soot.

JAMES DICKEY

(1923–)

The Performance

The last time I saw Donald Armstrong
He was staggering oddly off into the sun,
Going down, of the Philippine Islands.
I let my shovel fall, and put that hand
Above my eyes, and moved some way to one side
That his body might pass through the sun,

And I saw how well he was not
Standing there on his hands,
On his spindle-shanked forearms balanced,
Unbalanced, with his big feet looming and waving
In the great, untrustworthy air
He flew in each night, when it darkened.

Dust fanned in scraped puffs from the earth
Between his arms, and blood turned his face inside out,
To demonstrate its suppleness
Of veins, as he perfected his role.
Next day, he toppled his head off
On an island beach to the south,

And the enemy's two-handed sword
Did not fall from anyone's hands
At that miraculous sight,
As the head rolled over upon
Its wide-eyed face, and fell
Into the inadequate grave

He had dug for himself, under pressure.
Yet I put my flat hand to my eyebrows
Months later, to see him again

In the sun, when I learned how he died,
And imagined him, there,
Come, judged, before his small captors,

Doing all his lean tricks to amaze them—
The back somersault, the kip-up—
And at last, the stand on his hands,
Perfect, with his feet together,
His head down, evenly breathing,
As the sun poured up from the sea

And the headsman broke down
In a blaze of tears, in that light
Of the thin, long human frame
Upside down in its own strange joy,
And, if some other one had not told him,
Would have cut off the feet

Instead of the head,
And if Armstrong had not presently risen
In kingly, round-shouldered attendance,
And then knelt down in himself
Beside his hacked, glittering grave, having done
All things in this life that he could.

The Enclosure

Down the track of a Philippine Island
We rode to the aircraft in trucks,
Going past an enclosure of women,
Those nurses from sick-tents,
With a fume of sand-dust at our backs.
We leapt to the tail-gate,
And drew back, then,
From the guards of the trembling compound,

Where the nailed wire sang like a jew's-harp,
And the women like prisoners paced.
In the dog-panting night-fighter climbing,
Held up between the engines like a child,
I rested my head on my hands;
The drained mask fell from my face.
I thought I could see
Through the dark and the heart-pulsing wire,

Their dungarees float to the floor,
And their light-worthy hair shake down
In curls and remarkable shapes
That the heads of men cannot grow,
And women stand deep in a ring
Of light, and whisper in panic unto us
To deliver them out
Of the circle of impotence, formed

As moonlight spins round a propeller,
Delicate, eternal, though roaring.
A man was suspended above them,
Outcrying the engines with lust.
He was carried away without damage,
And the women, inviolate, woke
In a cloud of gauze,
Overhearing the engines' matched thunder.

Then, the voice of the man, inmixed,
Seemed to them reassuring, unheard-of,
Passing out softly into the hush
Of nipa-leaves, reeds and the sea,
And the long wind up from the beaches,
All making the nets to be trembling
Purely around them,
And fading the desperate sound

To the whine of mosquitoes, turned back
By the powdery cloth that they slept in,
Not touching it, sleeping or waking,
With a thing, not even their hair.
The man sat away in the moonlight,
In a braced, iron, kingly chair,
As the engines labored
And carried him off like a child

To the west, and the thunderstruck mainland.
It may have been the notion of a circle
Of light, or the sigh of the never-thumbed wire,
Or a cry with the shape of propellers,
Or the untouched and breath-trembling nets,
That led me later, at peace,
To shuck off my clothes
In a sickness of moonlight and patience,

With a tongue that cried low, like a jew's-harp,
And a white gaze shimmered upon me
Like an earthless moon, as from women
Sleeping kept from themselves, and beyond me,
To sweat as I did, to the north:
To pray to a skylight of paper, and fall
On the enemy's women
With intact and incredible love.

The Firebombing

Denke daran, dass nach den grossen
   Zerstörungen
Jedermann beweisen wird, dass er
   unshuldig war.
                     —Günter Eich
Or hast thou an arm like God?
                     —The Book of Job

Homeowners unite.

All families lie together, though some are burned alive.
The others try to feel
For them. Some can, it is often said.

Starve and take off

Twenty years in the suburbs, and the palm trees willingly leap
Into the flashlights,
And there is beneath them also
A booted crackling of snailshells and coral sticks.
There are cowl flaps and the tilt cross of propellers,
The shovel-marked clouds' far sides against the moon,
The enemy filling up the hills
With ceremonial graves. At my somewhere among these,

Snap, a bulb is tricked on in the cockpit

And some technical-minded stranger with my hands
Is sitting in a glass treasure-hole of blue light,
Having potential fire under the undeodorized arms
Of his wings, on thin bomb-shackles,
The "tear-drop-shaped" 300-gallon drop-tanks
Filled with napalm and gasoline.

Thinking forward ten minutes
From that, there is also the burst straight out

Of the overcast into the moon; there is now
The moon-metal-shine of propellers, the quarter-
moonstone, aimed at the waves,
Stopped on the cumulus.

There is then this re-entry
Into cloud, for the engines to ponder their sound.
In white dark the aircraft shrinks; Japan

Dilates around it like a thought.
Coming out, the one who is here is over
Land, passing over the all-night grainfields,
In dark paint over
The woods with one silver side,
Rice-water calm at all levels
Of the terraced hill.
                        Enemy rivers and trees
Sliding off me like snakeskin,
Strips of vapor spooled from the wingtips
Going   invisible   passing   over   on
Over   bridges   roads for nightwalkers
Sunday night in the enemy's country   absolute
Calm   the moon's face   coming   slowly
About
            the inland sea
Slants   is woven with wire thread
Levels out   holds together like a quilt
Off the starboard wing   cloud flickers
At my glassed-off forehead   the moon's now and again
Uninterrupted face going forward
Over the waves in a glide-path
Lost into land.

Going: going with it

Combat booze by my side in a cratered canteen,
Bourbon frighteningly mixed
With GI pineapple juice,
Dogs trembling under me for hundreds of miles, on many
Islands, sleep-smelling that ungodly mixture
Of napalm and high-octane fuel,
Good bourbon and GI juice.

Rivers circling behind me around
Come to the fore, and bring
A town with everyone darkened.
Five thousand people are sleeping off
An all-day American drone.
Twenty years in the suburbs have not shown me
Which ones were hit and which not.

Haul on the wheel   racking slowly
The aircraft blackly around
In a dark dream   that   that is
That is like flying inside someone's head

Think of this   think of this

I did not think of my house
But think of my house now

Where the lawn mower rests on its laurels
Where the diet exists
For my own good   where I try to drop
Twenty years, eating figs in the pantry
Blinded by each and all
Of the eye-catching cans that gladly have caught my wife's eye
Until I cannot say
Where the screwdriver is   where the children
Get off the bus   where the new
Scoutmaster lives   where the fly
Hones his front legs   where the hammock folds
Its erotic daydreams   where the Sunday
School text for the day has been put   where the fire
Wood is   where the payments
For everything under the sun
Pile peacefully up,

But in this half-paid-for pantry
Among the red lids that screw off
With an easy half-twist to the left
And the long drawers crammed with dim spoons,
I still have charge—secret charge—
Of the fire developed to cling
To everything: to golf carts and fingernail

Scissors as yet unborn   tennis shoes
Grocery baskets   toy fire engines
New Buicks stalled by the half-moon
Shining at midnight on crossroads   green paint
Of jolly garden tools   red Christmas ribbons:

Not atoms, these, but glue inspired
By love of country to burn,
The apotheosis of gelatin.

Behind me having risen the Southern Cross
Set up by chaplains in the Ryukyus—
Orion, Scorpio, the immortal silver
Like the myths of king-
insects at swarming time—
One mosquito, dead drunk
On altitude, drones on, far under the engines,
And bites between
The oxygen mask and the eye.
The enemy-colored skin of families
Determines to hold its color
In sleep, as my hand turns whiter
Than ever, clutching the toggle—
The ship shakes   bucks
Fire hangs   not yet fire
In the air above Beppu
For I am fulfilling

An "anti-morale" raid upon it.
All leashes of dogs
Break under the first bomb, around those
In bed, or late in the public baths: around those
Who inch forward on their hands
Into medicinal waters.
Their heads come up with a roar
Of Chicago fire:
Come up with the carp pond showing
The bathhouse upside down,
Standing stiller to show it more
As I sail artistically over
The resort town followed by farms,
Singing and twisting

All the handles in heaven   kicking
The small cattle off their feet
In a red costly blast
Flinging jelly over the walls
As in a chemical war-
fare field demonstration.
With fire of mine like a cat

Holding onto another man's walls,
My hat should crawl on my head
In streetcars, thinking of it,
The fat on my body should pale.

Gun down
The engines, the eight blades sighing
For the moment when the roofs will connect
Their flames, and make a town burning with all
American fire.
                              Reflections of houses catch;
Fire shuttles from pond to pond
In every direction, till hundreds flash with one death.
With this in the dark of the mind,
Death will not be what it should;
Will not, even now, even when
My exhaled face in the mirror
Of bars, dilates in a cloud like Japan.
The death of children is ponds
Shutter-flashing; responding mirrors; it climbs
The terraces of hills
Smaller and smaller, a mote of red dust
At a hundred feet; at a hundred and one it goes out.
That is what should have got in
To my eye
And shown the insides of houses, the low tables
Catch fire from the floor mats,
Blaze up in gas around their heads
Like a dream of suddenly growing
Too intense for war. Ah, under one's dark arms
Something strange-scented falls—when those on earth
Die, there is not even sound;
One is cool and enthralled in the cockpit,

Turned blue by the power of beauty,
In a pale treasure-hole of soft light
Deep in aesthetic contemplation,
Seeing the ponds catch fire
And cast it through ring after ring
Of land: O death in the middle
Of acres of inch-deep water!   Useless

Firing   small arms
Speckles   from the river
Bank   one ninety-millimeter
Misses   far down   wrong petals   gone

It is this detachment,
The honored aesthetic evil,
The greatest sense of power in one's life,
That must be shed in bars, or by whatever
Means, by starvation
Visions in well-stocked pantries:
The moment when the moon sails in between
The tail-booms   the rudders nod   I swing
Over   directly over the heart
The *heart* of the fire. A mosquito burns out on my cheek
With the cold of my face   there are the eyes
In blue light   bar light
All masked but them   the moon
Crossing from left to right   in the streams below
Oriental fish form quickly
In the chemical shine,
In their eyes one tiny seed
Of deranged, Old Testament light.

Letting go   letting go
The plane rises gently   dark forms
Glide off me   long water   pales
In safe zones   a new cry enters
The voice box of chained family dogs

We buck   leap over something
Not there   settle back
Leave it   leave it clinging and crying

It consumes them in a hot
Body-flash, old age or menopause
Of children, clings and burns
                    eating through
And when a reed mat catches fire
From me, it explodes through field after field
Bearing its sleeper   another

Bomb finds a home
And clings to it like a child. And so

Goodbye to the grassy mountains
To cloud streaming from the night engines
Flags   pennons   curved silks
Of air   myself streaming also
My body covered
With flags, the air of flags
Between the engines.
Forever I do sleep in that position,
Forever in a turn
For home that breaks out streaming banners
From my wingtips,
Wholly in position to admire.

O then I knock it off
And turn for home over the black complex thread worked through
The silver night-sea,
Following the huge, moon-washed steppingstones
Of the Ryukyus south,
The nightgrass of mountains billowing softly
In my rising heat.
                    Turn and tread down
The yellow stones of the islands
To where Okinawa burns,
Pure gold, on the radar screen,
Beholding, beneath, the actual island form
In the vast water-silver poured just above solid ground,
An inch of water extending for thousands of miles
Above flat ploughland. Say "down," and it is done.

All this, and I am still hungry,
Still twenty years overweight, still unable

To get down there or see
What really happened.
                              But it may be that I could not,
If I tried, say to any
Who lived there, deep in my flames: say, in cold
Grinning sweat, as to another
As these homeowners who are always curving
Near me down the different-grassed street: say
As though to the neighbor
I borrowed the hedge-clippers from
On the darker-grassed side of the two,
Come in, my house is yours, come in
If you can, if you
Can pass this unfired door. It is that I can imagine
At the threshold nothing
With its ears crackling off
Like powdery leaves,
Nothing with children of ashes, nothing not
Amiable, gentle, well-meaning,
A little nervous for no
Reason   a little worried   a little too loud
Or too easygoing   nothing I haven't lived with
For twenty years, still nothing not as
American as I am, and proud of it.

Absolution? Sentence? No matter;
The thing itself is in that.

Drinking from a Helmet

I

I climbed out, tired of waiting
For my foxhole to turn in the earth
On its side or its back for a grave,
And got in line
Somewhere in the roaring of dust.
Every tree on the island was nowhere,
Blasted away.

II

In the middle of combat, a graveyard
Was advancing after the troops
With laths and balls of string;
Grass already tinged it with order.
Between the new graves and the foxholes
A green water-truck stalled out.
I moved up on it, behind
The hill that cut off the firing.

III

My turn, and I shoved forward
A helmet I picked from the ground,
Not daring to take mine off
Where somebody else may have come
Loose from the steel of his head.

IV

Keeping the foxhole doubled
In my body and begging

For water, safety, and air,
I drew water out of the truckside
As if dreaming the helmet full.
In my hands, the sun
Came on in a feathery light.

V

In midair, water trimming
To my skinny dog-faced look
Showed my life's first all-out beard
Growing wildly, escaping from childhood,
Like the beards of the dead, all now
Underfoot beginning to grow.
Selected ripples wove through it,
Knocked loose with a touch from all sides
Of a brain killed early that morning,
Most likely, and now
In its absence holding
My sealed, sunny image from harm,
Weighing down my hands,
Shipping at the edges,
Too heavy on one side, then the other.

VI

I drank, with the timing of rust.
A vast military wedding
Somewhere advanced one step.

VII

All around, equipment drifting in light,
Men drinking like cattle and bushes,
Cans, leather, canvas and rifles,
Grass pouring down from the sun
And up from the ground.
Grass: and the summer advances

Invisibly into the tropics.
Wind, and the summer shivers
Through many men standing or lying
In the GI gardener's hand
Spreading and turning green
All over the hill.

VIII

At the middle of water
Bright circles dawned inward and outward
Like oak rings surviving the tree
As its soul, or like
The concentric gold spirit of time.
I kept trembling forward through something
Just born of me.

IX

My nearly dead power to pray
Like an army increased and assembled,
As when, in a harvest of sparks,
The helmet leapt from the furnace
And clamped itself
On the heads of a billion men.
Some words directed to Heaven
Went through all the strings of the graveyard
Like a message that someone sneaked in,
Tapping a telegraph key
At dead of night, then running
For his life.

X

I swayed, as if kissed in the brain.
Above the shelled palm-stumps I saw
How the tops of huge trees might be moved
In a place in my own country

I never had seen in my life.
In the closed dazzle of my mouth
I fought with a word in the water
To call on the dead to strain
Their muscles to get up and go there.
I felt the difference between
Sweat and tears when they rise,
Both trying to melt the brow down.

XI

On even the first day of death
The dead cannot rise up,
But their last thought hovers somewhere
For whoever finds it.
My uninjured face floated strangely
In the rings of a bodiless tree.
Among them, also, a final
Idea lived, waiting
As in Ariel's limbed, growing jail.

XII

I stood as though I possessed
A cool, trembling man
Exactly my size, swallowed whole.
Leather swung at his waist,
Web-cord, buckles, and metal,
Crouching over the dead
Where they waited for all their hands
To be connected like grass-roots.

XIII

In the brown half-life of my beard
The hair stood up
Like the awed hair lifting the back
Of a dog that has eaten a swan.

Now light like this
Staring into my face
Was the first thing around me at birth.
Be no more killed, it said.

XIV

The wind in the grass
Moved gently in secret flocks,
Then spread to be
Nothing, just where they were.
In delight's
Whole shining condition and risk,
I could see how my body might come
To be imagined by something
That thought of it only for joy.

XV

Fresh sweat and unbearable tears
Drawn up by my feet from the field
Between my eyebrows became
One thing at last,
And I could cry without hiding.
The world dissolved into gold;
I could have stepped up into air.
I drank and finished
Like tasting of Heaven,
Which is simply of,
At seventeen years,
Not dying wherever you are.

XVI

Enough
Shining, I picked up my carbine and said.
I threw my old helmet down
And put the wet one on.
Warmed water ran over my face.

My last thought changed, and I knew
I inherited one of the dead.

XVII

I saw tremendous trees
That would grow on the sun if they could,
Towering. I saw a fence
And two boys facing each other,
Quietly talking,
Looking in at the gigantic redwoods,
The rings in the trunks turning slowly
To raise up stupendous green.
They went away, one turning
The wheels of a blue bicycle,
The smaller one curled catercornered
In the handlebar basket.

XVIII

I would survive and go there,
Stepping off the train in a helmet
That held a man's last thought,
Which showed him his older brother
Showing him trees.
I would ride through all
California upon two wheels
Until I came to the white
Dirt road where they had been,
Hoping to meet his blond brother,
And to walk with him into the wood
Until we were lost,
Then take off the helmet
And tell him where I had stood,
What poured, what spilled, what swallowed:

XIX

And tell him I was the man.

DONALD W. BAKER

(*1923–*)

Delinquent Elegy

for Keith Douglas

John Smith (1923–1944)

My friend John Smith, a usual man,
urging his bomber from the earth,
heard his life end in a loud bang
and took fire with his last breath.

Our engines idled through the necessary pause,
until his passion was extinguished.
Then the others of the squadron rose
into the morning, over John Smith's ashes,

bombed, and at noon returned, most of them,
to the hut where, with one dropping eye,
the colonel drew the obvious lesson:
how not to fly.

No day could have been more ordinary.
So much was burning in that bad time
that no one troubled to sing an elegy
for John Smith and his crew of nine.

That was almost forty years ago.
Now in the evening on our TV
the shining bombers climb and show
us how it was, is, and again will be,

while here, where only a desk lamp burns,
I rake old anguish to make my truth
and record at last some ordinary rhymes,
a late song for a long-dead youth,

my friend John Smith, who, in the Second War,
blew up and burned, one among many,
a clownish hero, killed by error,
as smart as most, as brave as any.

ALAN DUGAN

(1923–)

Portrait from the Infantry

He smelled bad and was red-eyed with the miseries
of being scared while sleepless when he said
this: "I want a private woman, peace and quiet,
and some green stuff in my pocket. Fuck
the rest." Pity the underwear and socks,
long burnt, of an accomplished murderer,
oh God, of germans and replacements, who
refused three stripes to keep his B.A.R.,
who fought, fought not to fight some days
like any good small businessman of war,
and dug more holes than an outside dog
to modify some Freudian's thesis: "No
man can stand three hundred days
of fear of mutilation and death." What he
theorized was a joke: "To keep a tight
ass-hole, dry socks and a you-deep hole
with you at all times." Afterwards,
met in a sports shirt with a round wife, he was
the clean slave of a daughter, a power brake
and beer. To me, he seemed diminished
in his dream, or else enlarged, who knows?,
by its accomplishment: personal life
wrung from mass issues in a bloody time
and lived out hiddenly. Aside from sound
baseball talk, his only interesting remark
was, in pointing to his wife's belly, "If
he comes out left foot first" (the way
you Forward March!), "I am going to stuff
him back up." "Isn't he awful?" she said.

LOUIS SIMPSON
(1923–)

Carentan O Carentan

Trees in the old days used to stand
And shape a shady lane
Where lovers wandered hand in hand
Who came from Carentan.

This was the shining green canal
Where we came two by two
Walking at combat-interval.
Such trees we never knew.

The day was early June, the ground
Was soft and bright with dew.
Far away the guns did sound,
But here the sky was blue.

The sky was blue, but there a smoke
Hung still above the sea
Where the ships together spoke
To towns we could not see.

Could you have seen us through a glass
You would have said a walk
Of farmers out to turn the grass,
Each with his own hay-fork.

The watchers in their leopard suits
Waited till it was time,
And aimed between the belt and boot
And let the barrel climb.

I must lie down at once, there is
A hammer at my knee.
And call it death or cowardice,
Don't count again on me.

Everything's all right, Mother,
Everyone gets the same
At one time or another.
It's all in the game.

I never strolled, nor ever shall,
Down such a leafy lane.
I never drank in a canal,
Nor ever shall again.

There is a whistling in the leaves
And it is not the wind,
The twigs are falling from the knives
That cut men to the ground.

Tell me, Master-Sergeant,
The way to turn and shoot.
But the Sergeant's silent
That taught me how to do it.

O Captain, show us quickly
Our place upon the map.
But the Captain's sickly
And taking a long nap.

Lieutenant, what's my duty,
My place in the platoon?
He too's a sleeping beauty,
Charmed by that strange tune.

Carentan O Carentan
Before we met with you
We never yet had lost a man
Or known what death could do.

The Battle

Helmet and rifle, pack and overcoat
Marched through a forest. Somewhere up ahead
Guns thudded. Like the circle of a throat
The night on every side was turning red.

They halted and they dug. They sank like moles
Into the clammy earth between the trees.
And soon the sentries, standing in their holes,
Felt the first snow. Their feet began to freeze.

At dawn the first shell landed with a crack.
Then shells and bullets swept the icy woods.
This lasted many days. The snow was black.
The corpses stiffened in their scarlet hoods.

Most clearly of that battle I remember
The tiredness in eyes, how hands looked thin
Around a cigarette, and the bright ember
Would pulse with all the life there was within.

Memories of a Lost War

The guns know what is what, but underneath
In fearful file
We go around burst boots and packs and teeth
That seem to smile.

The scene jags like a strip of celluloid,
A mortar fires,
Cinzano falls, Michelin is destroyed,
The man of tires.

As darkness drifts like fog in from the sea
Somebody says
"We're digging in." Look well, for this may be
The last of days.

Hot lightnings stitch the blind eye of the moon,
The thunder's blunt.
We sleep. Our dreams pass in a faint platoon
Toward the front.

Sleep well, for you are young. Each tree and bush
Drips with sweet dew,
And earlier than morning June's cool hush
Will waken you.

The riflemen will wake and hold their breath.
Though they may bleed
They will be proud a while of something death
Still seems to need.

The Bird

"*Ich wünscht', ich wäre ein Vöglein,*"
Sang Heinrich, "I would fly
Across the sea . . ." so sadly
It made his mother cry.

At night he played his zither,
By day worked in the mine.
His friend was Hans; together
The boys walked by the Rhine.

"Each day we're growing older,"
Hans said, "This is no life.
I wish I were a soldier!"
And snapped his pocketknife.

War came, and Hans was taken,
But Heinrich did not fight.
"*Ich wünscht', ich wäre ein Vöglein,*"
Sang Heinrich every night.

"Dear Heinrich," said the letter,
"I hope this finds you fine.
The war could not be better,
It's women, song and wine."

A letter came for Heinrich,
The same that he'd sent East
To Hans, his own handwriting
Returned, and marked *Deceased.*

*

"You'll never be a beauty,"
The doctor said, "You scamp!
We'll give you special duty—
A concentration camp."

And now the truck was nearing
The place. They passed a house;
A radio was blaring
The *Wiener Blut* of Strauss.

The banks were bright with flowers,
The birds sang in the wood;
There was a fence with towers
On which armed sentries stood.

They stopped. The men dismounted;
Heinrich got down—at last!
"That chimney," said the sergeant,
"That's where the Jews are gassed."

*

Each day he sorted clothing,
Skirt, trousers, boot and shoe,
Till he was filled with loathing
For every size of Jew.

"Come in! What is it, Private?"
"Please Sir, that vacancy . . .
I wonder, could I have it?"
"Your papers! Let me see . . .

"You're steady and you're sober . . .
But have you learned to kill?"
Said Heinrich, "No, *Herr Ober-
Leutnant*, but I will!"

"The Reich can use your spirit.
Report to Unit Four.
Here is an arm-band—wear it!
Dismissed! Don't slam the door."

*

"*Ich wünscht', ich wäre ein Vöglein,*"
Sang Heinrich, "I would fly . . ."
They knew that when they heard him
The next day they would die.

They stood in silence praying
At midnight when they heard
The zither softly playing,
The singing of the Bird.

He stared into the fire,
He sipped a glass of wine.
"*Ich wünscht'*," his voice rose higher,
"*Ich wäre ein Vöglein* . . ."

A dog howled in its kennel,
He thought of Hans and cried.
The stars looked down from heaven.
That day the children died.

*

"The Russian tanks are coming!"
The wind bore from the east
A cannonade, a drumming
Of small arms that increased.

Heinrich went to Headquarters.
He found the Colonel dead
With pictures of his daughters,
A pistol by his head.

He thought, his courage sinking,
"There's always the SS . . ."
He found the Major drinking
In a woman's party dress.

The prisoners were shaking
Their barracks. Heinrich heard
A sound of timber breaking,
A shout, "Where is the Bird?"

*

The Russian was completing
A seven-page report.
He wrote: "We still are beating
The woods . . ." then he stopped short.

A little bird was flitting
Outside, from tree to tree.
He turned where he was sitting
And watched it thoughtfully.

He pulled himself together,
And wrote: "We've left no stone
Unturned—but not a feather!
It seems the Bird has flown.

"Description? Half a dozen
Group snapshots, badly blurred;
And which is Emma's cousin
God knows, and which the Bird!

"He could be in the Western
Or in the Eastern Zone.
I'd welcome a suggestion
If anything is known."

*

"*Ich wünscht', ich wäre ein Vöglein,*"
Sings Heinrich, "I would fly
Across the sea," so sadly
It makes his children cry.

On the Ledge

I can see the coast coming near . . .
one of our planes, a Thunderbolt, plunging down
and up again. Seconds later
we heard the rattle of machine guns.

That night we lay among hedgerows.
The night was black. There was thrashing
in a hedgerow, a burst of firing . . .
in the morning, a dead cow.

A plane droned overhead . . .
one of theirs,
diesel, with a rhythmic sound.
Then the bombs came whistling down.

*

We were strung out on an embankment
side by side in a straight line,
like infantry in World War One
waiting for the whistle to blow.

The Germans knew we were there
and were firing everything they had,
bullets passing right above.
I knew that in a moment the order would come.

There is a page in Dostoevsky
about a man being given the choice
to die, or to stand on a ledge
through all eternity . . .

alive and breathing the air,
looking at the trees, and sky . . .
the wings of a butterfly
as it drifts from stem to stem.

But men who have stepped off the ledge
know all that there is to know:
who survived the Bloody Angle,
Verdun, the first day on the Somme.

As it turned out, we didn't have to.
Instead, they used Typhoons.
They flew over our heads, firing rockets
on the German positions.

So it was easy. We just strolled
over the embankment,
and down the other side,
and across an open field.

Yet, like the man on the ledge,
I still haven't moved . . .
watching an ant
climb a blade of grass and climb back down.

A Bower of Roses

The mixture of smells—
of Algerian tobacco,
wine barrels, and urine—
I'll never forget it,
he thought, if I live to be a hundred.

And the whores in every street,
and like flies in the bars . . .
Some of them looked familiar:
there was a Simone Simone,
a Veronica.

And some were original,
like the two who stood on a corner,
a brunette with hair like ink
and a platinum blonde,
holding a Great Dane on a leash.

"A monster," said Margot.
"Those three give me the shivers."

The other girls were of the same opinion.
One said, "And, after all,
think what a dog like that must cost to feed."

This was conclusive. They stared out at the street—
there was nothing more to be said.

*

When they gave him a pass at the hospital
he would make for the bar in Rue Sainte Apolline
Margot frequented. Sitting in a corner
as though she had been waiting . . .

Like the sweetheart on a postcard
gazing from a bower of roses . . .
"Je t'attends toujours."

For ten thousand francs
she would let him stay the night,
and a thousand for the concièrge.
The maid, too, must have something.

Then, finally, he would be alone with her.
Her face a perfect oval,
a slender neck, brown hair . . .

It surprised him that a girl
who looked delicate in her clothes
was voluptuous when she stood naked.

*

He caught up with the division in Germany,
at Dusseldorf, living in houses
a hundred yards from the Rhine.

Now and then a shell flew over.
For every shell Krupp fired
General Motors sent back four.

Division found some cases of beer,
and cigars, and passed them around—
a taste of the luxury
that was coming. The post-war.

One morning they crossed the Rhine.
Then they were marching through villages
where the people stood and stared.
Then they rode in convoys of trucks
on the autobahns. Deeper in.

The areas on the map of Germany
marked with the swastika kept diminishing,
and then, one day, there were none left.

*

They were ordered back to France,
only sixty kilometers from Paris.

Once more he found himself climbing the stairs.
He knocked, and heard footsteps.
"Who is it?"
              The door opened a crack,
then wide, and he was holding her.
"My God," she said, "chéri,
I never thought to see you again."

That night, lying next to her,
he thought about young women
he had known back in the States
who would not let you do anything.
And a song of the first war . . .
"How Are You Going to Keep Them Down on the Farm?
(After They've Seen Paree)."

He supposed this was what life taught you,
that words you thought were a joke,
and applied to someone else,
were real, and applied to you.

RICHARD HUGO
(1923–1982)

Mission to Linz

I

If you look at the sky
north, there where it ends
as if finite or breaks its northern orange,
in a vacuum of time
you might suddenly know this:
that the sky where it ends does not end
and you will pass its horizons.

You must know it before
you can think of it, speak of it;
it must come on you more sudden than flare
before you identify yourself with the power:
the olive with yellow band death in the bay,
the Pratts, the Hamilton Standards,
the Norden, turrets of fifty calibers.

It must seem weird, incommunicable
the desire for ozone
cold and the unremembered terrible.

You could realize an angel in orange
between the Alps, blue in summer, and the spray of cirrus
but that is visual and will not do
and besides it is remembered beautiful.

Or you might hear the rotation to come,
the thunder of revolving iron,
the padded burst blackening under the nose,
sound of the almighty sickening

but that is auditory and will not do
and besides it is remembered terrible.

You can see the gunners smoking
on the morning stones.
The navigator tugging his harness.
The pilot who checks everything twice.
The good-natured bombardier
or co-pilot swearing.
They too could look at the sky
north, there where it ends
as if finite or breaks its northern orange,
and in that moment of no time know it:
where they will be in hours
of rotation and revolving iron
before they can think of it,
speak of it.

It must seem weird, incommunicable
the desire for ozone
cold and the unremembered terrible.

You can know it.
It will come on you quickly.
But even if you can say it,
once the engines have started nothing is heard.

2

Nothing is heard in the north,
and the northern temperatures grow cold with the height.
There is the stark crack of voice
taking oxygen checks and the sharp static answers.
You are beyond birds, a season called summer.
There are places away from the world where the air is always
        winter.
Nothing is heard in the north.

The engines pound out their particular fever
a sound that has a silence of its own.
There is the control of needles and gauges, green

and showing the speed, the degrees and the climb,
and the six boxes of six shudder and rock
where the sun goes pale in the thinness of air
above the Adriatic. Fifties are tested,
checked in
with the stark crack of six voices
and the seventh replying with a sharp static answer.
And the engines pound out their particular fever
a sound that has a silence of its own.

No one can call this movement
though Europe wavers and falls back to the south
and a needle says one-fifty-four. The air
is ten centuries of waiting. A flange
is your breathing and the throat says nothing
behind the tight mask, and the mask,
the silent engines are all your loss of self.

The sterile Alps, blue in summer
swing up, pass for an hour underneath,
fall harshly into their brown valleys
and the grey one rail towns of vertical protection.

But what do you think
while Europe wavers and falls back to the south
in a way that is not called movement?
While the flange breathes for you
and the needles swing to other numbers?

Europe wavers and falls back to the south,
the silence rotates your life in the roar
and you think this:
that out of thirty-six we stand a chance
(statistic) to lose three at the most.
Twenty minutes before the wide turn
you will say it over and over
where the air is twenty centuries of tension
and the sun goes pale in the thinness of air
you will say it: three at the most.

But the engines pound out their particular fever.
A silence of its own.

There are places away from the world where the air is always
     winter.
Nothing is heard in the north.

                              3

You fly north to a point, swing slowly
to the east, open your belly and brace
before the eight-minute course, planned
on violet maps a smile before, but now
Linz opens like a flower below your nose
and the silence drives louder airs into the bay.
The dagger black explodes and the praying increases
until the over-ripe melon of day, cracking its hide
shows the red-moist fear just back of your brows.

A plane evaporates so quickly,
silently, it might have been
from magic were it not your fear
knew ten reduced molecular.
There is the silence and the waiting
in eight-minute vacuum, and black puffing
thick as enormous dark rain,
some, the close, sounding, a few
the very close, jolting.

Out of the thirty-five still airborne
there was a moment, one
your dreams will lose, stopped in tiny fire,
flipped dizzily away,
a wing peeled back like a sudden unloosening arm
fluttered down five miles of sky as paper,
and you didn't hear a thing.

And the moment
when the sky split open, allowed
the lazy tons of yellow-banded children
to fall in forty-second wonder, converge
in a giant funnel. Now you
who, so high, can only see
the puff like a penny dropped in dust

at your toe on a country road, rack up
and out, down with a speed
that strains the blueprint—until
noiselessness, the level back
into clean sky.

Of all this, this, and only it:
you can forget, and will, the degrading prayer
when the sound is gone, only this:
you feel good to your own touch,
you remain.

4

Summer is heard in the south,
and the southern temperatures grow warm as you drop.
The speed is easier, the brain
warmed by the sound of insult,
and you defend yourself by making fun
of others' fear, of your own prayers.
You come into birds, a sun that is warmer.
There is land away from the sky where the sound is always
        summer.

There is the needle control, the green gauges
showing the speed, the degrees and the fall.
The engines sing you to the home of men,
the earth, and think of it; its brownness,
its solidity, its greenness. You can build
warm rooms on its hills, love on it,
and if you die on it you remain
long enough to be lied about, buried in it.

Anyone can call this movement.
Europe speeds back to the north. The Adriatic
glimmers its blues to the brown shores of summer
and the engines sing you to the home of men,
the earth, and think of it.

If you think of it you know soil
is its own loveliness and you want to be on it
to drink, speak and study friends' faces.

If you think about it for a long time
the mind, like engines, will sing
you to the home of men,
where concerts carry
fast in summer wind.

Where We Crashed

I was calling airspeed
christ
one-thirty-five and
pancake bam
glass going first
breaking slow
slow dream
breaking
slow
sliding
gas and bombs
sliding
you end
now
here
explode
damn
damn
Steinberg
pilot
should
have found
more sky
you end
here
boom
now
boom
gone
no more
gone
good-bye
bye bye
boom
go boom
piled on
into panel

from behind
off
off
swinging
tire loose
strut caught
slow circle
turn
swinging
ripping
gas and bombs
aluminum
hole open
out
sweet
cheese-eating
jesus
out
clumsy
nothing
fuckass
nothing
shithead
nothing
moldy
cunteyed
bastard
nothing
stuck
shove
him
prick
jump
run
sweet
cheese-eating
jesus
run
gas
bombs
running
rain

faint rain
running
farmer
screaming
something
someone
·45
shoot
get back
shoot him back
gas and bombs
running
Stewart
R.O.
Klamath Falls
out
he's out
on the horizon
running
live
O'Brien
L.A.
broken foot
limping
away
all away
from gas
from bombs
Knapp
ball turret
joking
farmer
yelling
Steinberg
staring gray
and in this grass
I didn't die

EDGAR BOWERS
(1924–)

The Stoic: for Laura von Courten

All winter long you listened for the boom
Of distant cannon wheeled into their place.
Sometimes outside beneath a bombers' moon
You stood alone to watch the searchlights trace

Their careful webs against the boding sky,
While miles away on Munich's vacant square
The bombs lunged down with an unruly cry
Whose blast you saw yet could but faintly hear.

And might have turned your eyes upon the gleam
Of a thousand years of snow, where near the clouds
The Alps ride massive to their full extreme,
And season after season glacier crowds

The dark, persistent smudge of conifers.
Or seen beyond the hedge and through the trees
The shadowy forms of cattle on the furze,
Their dim coats white with mist against the freeze.

Or thought instead of other times than these,
Of other countries and of other sights:
Eternal Venice sinking by degrees
Into the very water that she lights;

Reflected in canals, the lucid dome
Of Maria dell' Salute at your feet,
Her triple spires disfigured by the foam.
Remembered in Berlin the parks, the neat

Footpaths and lawns, the clean spring foliage,
Where just short weeks before, a bomb, unaimed,
Released a frightened lion from its cage,
Which in the mottled dark that trees enflamed

Killed one who hurried homeward from the raid.
And by yourself there standing in the chill
You must, with so much known, have been afraid
And chosen such a mind of constant will,

Which, though all time corrode with constant hurt,
Remains, until it occupies no space,
That which it is; and passionless, inert,
Becomes at last no meaning and no place.

Clothes

—Bavaria, 1946

Walking back to the office after lunch,
I saw Hans. "Mister Isham, Mister Isham,"
He called out in his hurry, "Herr Wegner needs you.
A woman waiting for a border pass
Took poison, she is dead, and the police
Are there to take the body." In the hall,
The secretaries stood outside their doors
Silently waiting with Wegner. "Sir," he said,
"It was her answer on the questionnaire,
A clerk for the Gestapo. So it was."
Within the outer office, by the row
Of wooden chairs, one lying on its side,
On the discolored brown linoleum floor
Under a GI blanket was the lost
Unmoving shape; uncovered, from a fold,
A dirty foot half out of a dirty shoe,
Once white, heel bent, the sole worn through, the skin
Bruised red and calloused, uncut toe nails curved
And veined like an old ivory. No one spoke.
Police stood at attention by a stretcher.
After an empty moment, suddenly
Bent over as if taken by a cramp,
I sobbed out loud and on my uniform
Vomited up my lunch—over the tie,
The polished buttons and insignia.
The little strips of color and the green
Eisenhower jacket with its Eagle patch,
The taut pants in a crease, the glistening jump boots—
Vomiting and still sobbing, like a child
Awakened in the night, and sick. Wegner and Hans
Held me, murmuring, "Ach, dear sir, the war
Is over and not over, such things happen."
While no one else moved, Frau Schmidt brought a towel
To clean me off before Hans walked me back,

My arm across his shoulders and I retelling
The story of how, near Zell am See, we found,
Hung from a tree in leaf, the final sack
Of bones, in rotted Wehrmacht green. In the house
An SS lord had furnished for his mistress,
Deep sofas, Persian rugs and velvet drapes,
Frau König took my clothes. In my own room,
Wearing the Gucci robe Bouchard had taken
From a fine house before we got to Ulm,
Instead of lying down to rest, I studied
The book I read for German with Frau Schmidt,
Goethe's *Italian Journey*. Through the window,
The Watchman's upper slopes were shadows, green
And purple with the afternoon, its snows
Melting, its double peaks the victory sign.

LUCIEN STRYK
(1924–)

Sniper

An inch to the left
and I'd be twenty years
of dust by now. I can't

walk under trees without
his muzzle tracks me.
He'd hit through branches,

leaves pinned to his shoulders
whistling. We searched him
everywhere—up trunks,

in caves, down pits. Then
one night, his island taken,
he stepped from jungle

shade, leaves still pinned
upon him glistening
in the projector's light,

and tiptoed round to watch
our show, a weary kid
strayed in from trick-or-treat.

The Face

Weekly at the start
of the documentary
on World War II

a boy's face, doomed,
sharply beautiful,
floats in the screen,

a dark balloon
above a field of barbs,
the stench of gas.

Whoever holds the
string
will not let go.

Watching War Movies

Always the same: watching
World War II movies on TV,
landing barges bursting onto

islands, my skin crawls—
heat, dust—the scorpion
bites again. How I deceived

myself. Certain my role would
not make me killer, my unarmed
body called down fire from

scarred hills. As life took
life, blood coursed into
one stream. I knew one day,

the madness stopped, I'd make
my pilgrimage to temples,
gardens, serene masters of

a Way which pain was bonding.
Atoms fuse, a mushroom cloud,
the movie ends. But I still

stumble under camouflage, near
books of tranquil Buddhas by the
screen. The war goes on and on.

Letter to Jean-Paul Baudot, at Christmas

Friend, on this sunny day, snow sparkling
everywhere, I think of you once more,
how many years ago, a child Resistance

fighter trapped by Nazis in a cave
with fifteen others, left to die, you became
a cannibal. Saved by Americans,

the taste of a dead comrade's flesh foul
in your mouth, you fell onto the snow
of the Haute Savoie and gorged to purge yourself,

somehow to start again. Each winter since
you were reminded, vomiting for days.
Each winter since you told me at the Mabillon,

I see you on the first snow of the year
spreadeagled, face buried in that stench.
I write once more, Jean-Paul, though you don't

answer, because I must: today men do far worse.
Yours in hope of peace, for all of us,
before the coming of another snow.

Rooms

I.

The casket under the rose
in the funeral parlor is not
where you live, my mother.

Garbling words for father,
sister, son, aunts, brother-
in-law, wife on an alien

stage, I enter a place high
above daffodils, hyacinths,
tulips of neighboring

gardens, where fire-scaled
butterflies wing free among
leaves, as you sit beside me

in tears at the old kitchen
table, dreading the moment I
leave, a young soldier off to

the Pacific in World War II.
I quietly touch your hand, promise
to take care, write often. In

foxholes, opening mail, I see
you daily, sending your life-line
of words from that room. On

my return, I let myself in to
surprise you sorting my letters
like charms on the bright

checkered cloth. This time
tears come with joy. So what
am I doing making my sermon

here? You are outside the window,
looking in, the monarch you
once made a poem, pure spirit,

wings carrying you above the
rose, to calm your children's,
and their children's, grief.

II.

Forward observers, fresh
from mission in the hills
of Okinawa, we crawl back

to our foxholes, under
a battle hymn of mortar
flak and fire, charged

with rumor that our president
has died. Ginger, always
skeptic, rubs his three-day

stubble, mutters—
"At least," "On the contrary,"
"Oh yeah!" Hopsi, the clown,

gulps *Aqua Velva* lotion in
despair. Weary, I lie
in my earth-room, just four

feet deep, rest on my
duffle, feeling the outline
of letters from home, Walt

Whitman's *Leaves of Grass*
under my head. I think
of other times, time that

might never be, cry out
for all the dead. As
howitzers split distance,

and the shells aim back, I
stare up wondering at my
roof of shrapnel and stars.

III.

Children's voices strain, round
on round, sweetly breathless,
follow their father, the troubador,

fiddling a chanty in Paris, outside
the church of St. Germain-des-Prés.
The crowd bravos, coins chime on

asphalt. Farther on, a trumpeter
passes his hat in an outdoor café,
where I turn down the street to

the Hôtel de Buci, stop once again
to look into the door. After
thirty-five years, how to explain

to a weary-faced clerk my need
to peer into a room, the size of
a closet, my home for two years

as a GI student back from war.
Trudging there, laden with books,
from the Sorbonne each night, I'd

prop on the sagging bed, back to
one wall, feet up on the other,
stare at the candle's soft flame

in the long dresser mirror. I'd
read through the dictionary, stalking
new words for verse scrawled on

used paper bags, old envelopes
airmailed from home, to the beat
of the asthmatic radiator. How I

would love to climb those stairs once
more, see where it all began. Making
a bold check, in the g's, for granadilla—

where visions of stigmata, nail marks,
thorns became a poem heavy with
may-pops, fruit of the passionflower.

EDWARD FIELD

(1924–)

World War II

It was over Target Berlin the flak shot up our plane
just as we were dumping bombs on the already smoking city
on signal from the lead bomber in the squadron.
The plane jumped again and again as the shells burst under us
sending jagged pieces of steel rattling through our fuselage.
I'll never understand
how none of us got ripped by those fragments.

Then, being hit, we had to drop out of formation right away
losing speed and altitude,
and when I figured out our course with trembling hands on the
    instruments
(I was navigator)
we set out on the long trip home to England
alone, with two of our four engines gone
and gas streaming out of holes in the wing tanks.
That morning at briefing
we had been warned not to go to nearby Poland
partly liberated then by the Russians,
although later we learned that another crew in trouble
had landed there anyway,
and patching up their plane somehow,
returned gradually to England
roundabout by way of Turkey and North Africa.
But we chose England, and luckily
the Germans had no fighters to send up after us then
for this was just before they developed their jet.
To lighten our load we threw out
guns and ammunition, my navigation books, all the junk
and made it over Holland
with a few goodbye fireworks from the shore guns.

Over the North Sea the third engine gave out
and we dropped low over the water.
The gas gauge read empty but by keeping the nose down
a little gas at the bottom of the tank sloshed forward
and kept our single engine going.
High overhead, the squadrons were flying home in formation
—the raids had gone on for hours after us.
Did they see us down there in our trouble?
We radioed our final position for help to come
but had no idea if anyone
happened to be tuned in and heard us,
and we crouched together on the floor
knees drawn up and head down
in regulation position for ditching;
listened as the engine stopped, a terrible silence,
and we went down into the sea with a crash,
just like hitting a brick wall,
jarring bones, teeth, eyeballs panicky.
Who would ever think water could be so hard?
You black out, and then come to
with water rushing in like a sinking-ship movie.

All ten of us started getting out of there fast:
There was a convenient door in the roof to climb out by,
one at a time. We stood in line,
water up to our thighs and rising.
The plane was supposed to float for twenty seconds
but with all those flak holes
who could say how long it really would?
The two life rafts popped out of the sides into the water
but one of them only half inflated
and the other couldn't hold everyone
although they all piled into it, except the pilot,
who got into the limp raft that just floated.
The radio operator and I, out last,
(Did that mean we were least aggressive, least likely to survive?)
we stood on the wing watching the two rafts
being swept off by waves in different directions.
We had to swim for it.
Later they said the cords holding rafts to plane
broke by themselves, but I wouldn't have blamed them
for cutting them loose, for fear

that by waiting the plane would go down
and drag them with it.

I headed for the overcrowded good raft
and after a clumsy swim in soaked heavy flying clothes
got there and hung onto the side.
The radio operator went for the half-inflated raft
where the pilot lay with water sloshing over him,
but he couldn't swim, even with his life vest on,
being from the Great Plains—
his strong farmer's body didn't know
how to wallow through the water properly
and a wild current seemed to sweep him farther off.
One minute we saw him on top of a swell
and perhaps we glanced away for a minute
but when we looked again he was gone—
just as the plane went down sometime around then
when nobody was looking.

It was midwinter and the waves were mountains
and the water ice water.
You could live in it twenty-five minutes
the Ditching Survival Manual said.
Since most of the crew were squeezed on my raft
I had to stay in the water hanging on.
My raft? It was their raft, they got there first so they would live.
Twenty-five minutes I had.
Live, live, I said to myself.
You've got to live.
There looked like plenty of room on the raft
from where I was and I said so
but they said no.
When I figured the twenty-five minutes were about up
and I was getting numb,
I said I couldn't hold on anymore,
and a little rat-faced boy from Alabama, one of the gunners,
got into the icy water in my place,
and I got on the raft in his.
He insisted on taking off his flying clothes
which was probably his downfall because even wet clothes are
        protection,
and then worked hard, kicking with his legs, and we all paddled,

to get to the other raft,
and we tied them together.
The gunner got in the raft with the pilot
and lay in the wet.
Shortly after, the pilot started gurgling green foam from his
        mouth—
maybe he was injured in the crash against the instruments—
and by the time we were rescued,
he and the little gunner were both dead.

That boy who took my place in the water
who died instead of me
I don't remember his name even.
It was like those who survived the death camps
by letting others go into the ovens in their place.
It was him or me, and I made up my mind to live.
I'm a good swimmer,
but I didn't swim off in that scary sea
looking for the radio operator when he was washed away.
I suppose, then, once and for all,
I chose to live rather than be a hero, as I still do today,
although at that time I believed in being heroic, in saving the
        world,
even if, when opportunity knocked,
I instinctively chose survival.

As evening fell the waves calmed down
and we spotted a boat, far off, and signaled with a flare gun,
hoping it was English not German.
The only two who cried on being found
were me and a boy from Boston, a gunner.
The rest of the crew kept straight faces.

It was a British air-sea rescue boat:
They hoisted us up on deck,
dried off the living and gave us whisky and put us to bed,
and rolled the dead up in blankets,
and delivered us all to a hospital on shore
for treatment or disposal.
None of us even caught cold, only the dead.

This was a minor accident of war:
Two weeks in a rest camp at Southport on the Irish Sea
and we were back at Grafton-Underwood, our base,
ready for combat again,
the dead crewmen replaced by living ones,
and went on hauling bombs over the continent of Europe,
destroying the Germans and their cities.

W. D. SNODGRASS

(1926–)

Ten Days Leave

He steps down from the dark train, blinking; stares
At trees like miracles. He will play games
With boys or sit up all night touching chairs.
Talking with friends, he can recall their names.

Noon burns against his eyelids, but he lies
Hunched in his blankets; he is half awake
But still lacks nerve to open up his eyes;
Supposing it were just his old mistake?

But no; it seems just like it seemed. His folks
Pursue their lives like toy trains on a track.
He can foresee each of his father's jokes
Like words in some old movie that's come back.

He is like days when you've gone some place new
To deal with certain strangers, though you never
Escape the sense in everything you do,
"We've done this all once. Have I been here, ever?"

But no; he thinks it must recall some old film, lit
By lives you want to touch; as if he'd slept
And must have dreamed this setting, peopled it,
And wakened out of it. But someone's kept

His dream asleep here like a small homestead
Preserved long past its time in memory
Of some great man who lived here and is dead.
They have restored his landscape faithfully:

The hills, the little houses, the costumes:
How real it seems! But he comes, wide awake,
A tourist whispering through the priceless rooms
Who must not touch things or his hand might break

Their sleep and black them out. He wonders when
He'll grow into his sleep so sound again.

"After Experience Taught Me . . ."

After experience taught me that all the ordinary
Surroundings of social life are futile and vain;

    I'm going to show you something very
    Ugly: someday, it might save your life.

Seeing that none of the things I feared contain
In themselves anything either good or bad

    What if you get caught without a knife;
    Nothing—even a loop of piano wire;

Excepting only in the effect they had
Upon my mind, I resolved to inquire

    Take the first two fingers of this hand;
    Fork them out—kind of a "V for Victory"—

Whether there might be something whose discovery
Would grant me supreme, unending happiness.

    And jam them into the eyes of your enemy.
    You have to do this hard. Very hard. Then press

No virtue can be thought to have priority
Over this endeavor to preserve one's being.

    Both fingers down around the cheekbone
    And setting your foot high into the chest

No man can desire to act rightly, to be blessed,
To live rightly, without simultaneously

    You must call up every strength you own
    And you can rip off the whole facial mask.

Wishing to be, to act, to live. He must ask
First, in other words, to actually exist.

And you, whiner, who wastes your time
Dawdling over the remorseless earth,
What evil, what unspeakable crime
Have you made your life worth?

Magda Goebbels

—30 April, 1945.

*(After Dr. Haase gave them shots of morphine,
Magda gave each child an ampule of potassium
cyanide from a spoon.)*

This is the needle that we give
Soldiers and children when they live
Near the front in primitive
     Conditions or real dangers;
This is the spoon we use to feed
Men trapped in trouble or in need,
When weakness or bad luck might lead
     Them to the hands of strangers.

This is the room where you can sleep
Your sleep out, curled up under deep
Layers of covering that will keep
     You safe till all harm's past.
This is the bed where you can rest
In perfect silence, undistressed
By noise or nightmares, as my breast
     Once held you soft but fast.

This is the Doctor who has brought
Your needle with your special shot
To quiet you; you won't get caught
     Off guard or unprepared.
I am your nurse who'll comfort you;
I nursed you, fed you till you grew
Too big to feed; now you're all through
     Fretting or feeling scared.

This is the glass tube that contains
Calm that will spread down through your veins
To free you finally from all pains
     Of going on in error.

This tiny pinprick sets the germ
Inside you that fills out its term
Till you can feel yourself grow firm
    Against all doubt, all terror.

Into this spoon I break the pill
That stiffens the unsteady will
And hardens you against the chill
    Voice of a world of lies.
This amber medicine implants
Steadfastness in your blood; this grants
Immunity from greed and chance,
    And from all compromise.

This is the serum that can cure
Weak hearts; these pure, clear drops insure
You'll face what comes and can endure
    The test; you'll never falter.
This is the potion that preserves
You in a faith that never swerves;
This sets the pattern of your nerves
    Too firm for you to alter.

I set this spoon between your tight
Teeth, as I gave you your first bite;
This satisfies your appetite
    For other nourishment.
Take this on your tongue; this do
Remembering your mother who
So loved her Leader she stayed true
    When all the others went,

When every friend proved false, in the
Delirium of treachery
On every hand, when even He
    Had turned His face aside.
He shut himself in with His whore;
Then, though I screamed outside His door,
Said He'd not see me anymore.
    They both took cyanide.

Open wide, now, little bird;
I who sang you your first word
Soothe away every sound you've heard
    Except your Leader's voice.
Close your eyes, now; take your death.
Once we slapped you to take breath.
Vengeance is mine, the Lord God saith
    And cancels each last choice.

Once, my first words marked out your mind;
Just as our Leader's phrases bind
All hearts to Him, building a blind
    Loyalty through the nation,
We shape you into a pure form.
Trapped, our best soldiers tricked the storm,
The Reds: those last hours, they felt warm
    Who stood fast to their station.

You needn't fear what your life meant;
You won't curse how your hours were spent;
You'll grow like your own monument
    To all things sure and good,
Fixed like a frieze in high relief
Of granite figures that our Chief
Accepts into His true belief,
    His true blood-brotherhood.

You'll never bite the hand that fed you,
Won't turn away from those that bred you,
Comforted your nights and led you
    Into the thought of virtue;
You won't be turned from your own bed;
Won't turn into that thing you dread;
No new betrayal lies ahead;
    Now no one else can hurt you.

Returned to Frisco, 1946

We shouldered like pigs along the rail to try
And catch that first gray outline of the shore
Of our first life. A plane hung in the sky
From which a girl's voice sang: ". . . you're home once more."

For that one moment, we were dulled and shaken
By fear. What could still catch us by surprise?
We had known all along we would be taken
By hawkers, known what authoritative lies

Would plan us as our old lives had been planned.
We had stood years and, then, scrambled like rabbits
Up hostile beaches; why should we fear this land
Intent on luxuries and its old habits?

A seagull shrieked for garbage. The Bay Bridge,
Busy with noontime traffic, rose ahead.
We would have liberty, the privilege
Of lingering over steak and white, soft bread

Served by women, free to get drunk or fight,
Free, if we chose, to blow in our back pay
On smart girls or trinkets, free to prowl all night
Down streets giddy with lights, to sleep all day,

Pay our own way and make our own selections;
Free to choose just what they meant we should;
To turn back finally to our old affections,
The ties that lasted and which must be good.

Off the port side, through haze, we could discern
Alcatraz, lavender with flowers. Barred,
The Golden Gate, fading away astern,
Stood like the closed gate of your own backyard.

DONALD HALL

(1928–)

The Man in the Dead Machine

High on a slope in New Guinea
the Grumman Hellcat
lodges among bright vines
as thick as arms. In 1942,
the clenched hand of a pilot
glided it here
where no one has ever been.

In the cockpit the helmeted
skeleton sits
upright, held
by dry sinews at neck
and shoulder, and webbing
that straps the pelvic cross
to the cracked
leather of the seat, and the breastbone
to the canvas cover
of the parachute.

Or say that the shrapnel
missed him, he flew
back to the carrier, and every
morning takes his chair, his pale
hands on the black arms, and sits
upright, held
by the firm webbing.

TURNER CASSITY
(1929–)

U-24 Anchors off New Orleans
(1938)

The only major city, one would hope,
Below the level of a periscope.
An air so wet, a sewer-damp so ill,
One had as well be under water still.

The muddy river cakes us, camouflages.
Maddened goats, my crew go off in barges.
At a distance—I do not refer
To feet and inches—I go too. To err

Defines the deckhands; not to is the Bridge.
Discretion is the sex of privilege.
The streetcars meet the levee four abreast;
I cleverly have picked the noisiest.

A mad mapmaker made this master plan,
To wring out, of his grid of streets, a fan.
One German restaurant, well meant but erring:
Ten kinds of shellfish; bouillabaisse; no herring.

Have my men fared better? Where they are
Becomes a high Weimar Republic bar.
There—lower Bourbonstrasse—lace and leather
Mingle in Louisiana weather.

Crack your whip, Old Harlot; pop your garter.
Who lives here is, by definition, martyr.
If I come back I'll think to pack libido.
For symbolism there will be torpedo.

MILLER WILLIAMS

(1930–)

Wiedersehen

When open trucks with German prisoners in them
passed in convoy through the small town
I dreamed in, my fourteenth year, of touchable breasts
and cars and the Cards and the Browns, we grabbed the shirts
we twisted and tied for bases and chased the trucks
past all our houses slow as we could run.

We tossed the baseball up to one of the guards
who sometimes pretended to keep it but threw it back.
Once I threw it badly. A German caught it.
A boy barely older than I was and blonder
and nearly as thin. He grinned and I thought how much
the baseball belonging to John Oscar Carpenter
must have cost. The guard didn't seem concerned
about the baseball or me. We ran for blocks
behind the flatbed truck. The side rails rattling
made the same sense the Germans did
calling and tossing the ball to one another.

We ran in silence needing our breath to breathe
and knowing that begging raises the value of things.
At the edge of town the convoy speeded up.
Everyone stopped but me and the truck pulled away.
I looked back once to see the seven others
standing on the curb of the last street
loose and surprised as a group on a picnic
looking into a river where someone has drowned.

When I turned back to the trucks, pumping my arms,
the pain in my side coming to punish me hard,
to burn the blame away and make us even,

even John Oscar Carpenter and I,
the young German hauled back and let the ball
fly in a flat arc from center field.
I caught it. I held it in the hand I waved
as truck by truck the convoy shifted gears.
"Wiedersehen," he yelled. A word I knew.
I turned and pegged the ball to home in time.
I wondered if he had killed the Rogers boy
or thrown the hand grenade at Luther Tackett
that blew his arm away. I had done something
nobody ever had done. It was large and frightful.
We walked in amazement a while and went to our houses.

Your grandchildren, German, do they believe the story,
the boy in Arkansas, blonder than you?

LARRY RUBIN

(1930–)

The Brother

(Note: For two years during World War II (1942–1944), the
Army Air Force Ground and Service Forces took over the luxury
hotels of Miami Beach as barracks; the soldiers trained in the
parks and on the beaches, and marched down the residential
streets of the city.)

I wore knee-pants there where the soldiers trained
Around the house, playing at war, and watched
Them dig up the beaches and park, and got a whiff
Of their fatigues as they marched past.
I never knew why Mother locked the door
At nine, but Sister's breasts rose past ribbons,
And she was proud outside the door. Knee-pants
At twelve, and all the soldiers laughed, but Sister
Made them hush. They dropped from sunlight
On parade, and she was there with ice and punch,
Sequins in the afternoon, flashing
Like helmets, or stars. I ladled, and she smiled,
And they were like the dead who rise through stones
Sighing for water, clutching her gift
Like battle gear. I grew there between them, gripping
The ladle, proud of her gown, waiting for war.

VAN K. BROCK
(1932–)

The Behaviorist

When they arrest you, you say, why me,
I've not done anything—
why my parents, my wife, my children.

They take you in trucks to trains.
After three days in cattlecars,
without water, and nauseous
from feces you've not yet learned
to recycle undigested parts of,
ingrained proprieties come to you
like Job's friends, saying,
"Had you not sinned, this could not be."
"God is just; this must be punishment."
The old syllogisms.

You perceive that those around you
must also be guilty, their suffering just:
when they put children in separate cars,
double deckers (for reeducation camps,
they said), you realize they will die
in transit, or on arrival.

One cooperates, accepts injustice as
necessary to greater justice, confesses,
begs forgiveness, proves oneself loyal,
worthier than those who will eat rats
before they acknowledge the rights
of raw power, despise those who do not see
your options, believe you had options.

You report the misconduct of fellow prisoners
and rise to the top like cream in a fetid room
absorbing the odors of the room.
The more you ingratiate yourself,
the more contempt you show those who won't learn.
You are a superior being.

The Faucets

. . . one or two per second   died
      just at Auschwitz. Not
a kitchen faucet's steady drip, but all faucets,
house and yard, suburbs and cities of Europe,
dripping at once:

Sachenhausen   Oranienburg   Dachau
    Lvov   Janowska,
Over 150 camps   Warsaw,
in Poland alone   Treblinka,
    Vilma,
not counting ghettos   Ponar,
starved burned machine-gunned   Kiev
buried alive in cavernous trenches   Babi Yar,
people funnelled
    Lublin,   Buchenwald,
worked   starved   Belsec,
    Sobibor,   Riga,
shipped in lots   Lodz,
    Minsk   Chelmno,
from Berlin, Amsterdam,   Maidanek,
    Belsen,   Bergen,
Prague, Paris, Vienna,   Ravensbruck,
    Auschwitz,   .
Budapest, Belgrade   Birkenau, .
    .   .
Bucharest, Athens   .   .
    .   .
the capitals and ghettos of Europe   to Auschwitz,
Wouldn't the Pope have broken with his plumber . . .
for such a loss? . .
Killed one or two per second just at Auschwitz. .
And less than one per minute on the whole Western Front.

JOHN N. MILLER

(1933–)

Windward of Hilo

When I was eight years old the war broke out.
We waited on the rocky, rain-drenched coast
Of Laupahoehoe, through two weeks of blackout,
Rumor, alert. Then troops came, set up post,
And sent a convoy batting out of hell
On a night supply run west toward Papaaloa.
With no lights, on wet pavement, a truck hurled
Straight off the snaky, cliff-edged road and fell
Ninety feet to a creek pool. Its two curled
Bodies wrapped in canvas brought the war
Home to our witness.
           Something in their hushed,
Hurried disposal drew us toward
That death-scene—four boys, furtive as we pushed
Up from the rocky beach, along the creek
Until our steep trail ended dead
Against sheer stone-cliff. There the pool lay, fed
By a thin waterfall, the truck
Already gone, but not its payload—glass
Shattered and gleaming, soft-drink cases strewn
Over the rocks.
         We traded stares, then splashed
Through mud and shallows for the few
Survivors, forced them open, sucked them dry.
Our tongues maintained the tang of cola
As we stole our way home, pledged to silence,
Knowing we owed our taste to the dead soldiers.

WALTER MCDONALD
(1934–)

The Winter They Bombed Pearl Harbor

The winter they bombed Pearl Harbor,
my brother finally let me follow
up the deepest snow drift in the town.
Each blizzard whipped between two homes

and piled dead-end on Joe Hall's shed,
long and low as a bunkhouse. Drifts
seemed like hills on plains so flat
I'd never seen a sled. In weeks,

my brother was off for war, and he dragged
and carried me up to the roof of the world.
Holding me high by one hand, he dropped me
like a flag up to my crotch in snow so soft

I believed if he let me go I'd sink.
There must have been something else
we did up there, Ed and his friends and me
the tag-along. But even if he let me fall

and had to tunnel down to save me,
if I sank, I can't recall. I've stared
and stared at these four pictures of us
like climbers, but nothing clicks. I'd like

to think I understood where he was going,
what war was and risk, and what
a brother meant. Even now, I try
to feel that afternoon, reach down my feet

on something solid I remember and hold
it all and turn it over like a snowball
in my mind, now that I'm old enough to value
loss, but I can't bring my brother back.

JAMES WHITEHEAD
(1936–)

He Remembers Something from the War

In Kansas during the war
   my grandfather made a big thing
   of a car left out in our alley—
There's bullet holes and human blood
   so hurry up and eat your supper.
And the whole world would jiggle a little
   like Jello, when he was nervous.
Mother and grandmother were gone
   to the movies to see my father winning
   the war in Europe—grandfather
   never went to the movies or church
   and for the same reasons.
This is a lot like the real trouble
   your father is having in Germany,
   he said, as we walked past our victory garden
   then down our alley.

The things themselves were plain—
   a blue Nash and a windbreaker
   stiff with blood
   but I wasn't scared
   even by the stain itself
   until he told the story
   about how for some reason
   a hitch-hiker had murdered a farmer
   then left the car and jacket in our alley
   after dumping out the dead farmer
   in the woods of northern Arkansas.
About the time the police arrived
   I asked why in our alley?

He was the only father I had
    those long years during the war
    my mother was gone to in the movies.

Later that night mother and grandmother
    scolded him for getting drunk
    because they didn't know the things
    behind the garden
    and wouldn't until the morning news
    that told another story
    which was a lie grandfather said,
    like Roosevelt.
Upstairs he staggered near the door
    outside my room and close to my bed
    where that night in a sweaty dream
    I saw a German soldier
    catching a ride
    with my own father
    in my own father's M-4 tank
    that was standing out in our alley.

C. K. WILLIAMS

(1936–)

Spit

> . . . then the son of the "superior race" began to spit into the Rabbi's
> mouth so that the Rabbi could continue to spit on the Torah . . .
>
> The Black Book

After this much time, it's still impossible. The SS man with his
    stiff hair and his uniform;
the Rabbi, probably in a torn overcoat, probably with a stained
    beard the other would be clutching;
the Torah, God's word, on the altar, the letters blurring under the
    blended phlegm;
the Rabbi's parched mouth, the SS man perfectly absorbed,
    obsessed with perfect humiliation.
So many years and what is there to say still about the soldiers
    waiting impatiently in the snow,
about the one stamping his feet, thinking, "Kill him! Get it over
    with!"
while back there the lips of the Rabbi and the other would have
    brushed
and if time had stopped you would have thought they were lovers,
so lightly kissing, the sharp, luger hand under the dear chin,
the eyes furled slightly and then when it started again the
    eyelashes of both of them
shyly fluttering as wonderfully as the pulse of a baby.
Maybe we don't have to speak of it at all, it's still the same.
War, that happens and stops happening but is always somehow
    right there, twisting and hardening us;
then what we make of God—words, spit, degradation, murder,
    shame; every conceivable torment.
All these ways to live that have something to do with how we live
and that we're almost ashamed to use as metaphors for what goes
    on in us

but that we do anyway, so that love is battle and we watch
ourselves in love
become maddened with pride and incompletion, and God is what
it is when we're alone
wrestling with solitude and everything speaking in our souls turns
against us like His fury
and just facing another person, there is so much terror and hatred
that yes,
spitting in someone's mouth, trying to make him defile his own
meaning,
would signify the struggle to survive each other and what we'll
enact to accomplish it.

There's another legend.
It's about Moses, that when they first brought him as a child
before Pharaoh
the king tested him by putting a diamond and a live coal in front
of him
and Moses picked up the red ember and popped it into his mouth
so for the rest of his life he was tongue-tied and Aaron had to
speak for him.
What must his scarred tongue have felt like in his mouth?
It must have been like always carrying something there that
weighed too much,
something leathery and dead whose greatest gravity was to loll out
like an ox's,
and when it moved, it must have been like a thick embryo slowly
coming alive,
butting itself against the inner sides of his teeth and cheeks.
And when God burned in the bush, how could he not cleave
to him?
How could he not know that all of us were on fire and that every
word we said would burn forever,
in pain, unquenchably, and God knew it, too, and would say
nothing Himself ever again beyond this,
ever, but would only live in the flesh that we use like firewood,
in all the caves of the body, the gut cave, the speech cave:
He would slobber and howl like something just barely a man that
beats itself again and again onto the dark,
moist walls away from the light, away from whatever would be
light for this last eternity.
"Now therefore go," He said, "and I will be with thy mouth."

GIBBONS RUARK
(1941–)

Sleeping Out with My Father

Sweet smell of earth and easy rain on
Canvas, small breath fogging up the lantern
Glass, and sleep sifting my bones, drifting me
Far from hide-and-seek in tangled hedges,
The chicken dinner with its hills of rice
And gravy and its endless prayers for peace,
Old ladies high above me creaking in the choir loft,
And then the dream of bombs breaks up my sleep,
The long planes screaming down the midnight
Till the whistles peel my skin back, the bombs
Shake up the night in a sea of lightning
And stench and spitting shrapnel and children
Broken in the grass, and I am running
Running with my father through the hedges
Down the flaming streets to fields of darkness,
To sleep in sweat and wake to news of war.

WILLIAM TROWBRIDGE
(1941–)

War Baby

When I was born
they had just gotten
the hang of it.
Mass production was the key,
industrial soap an unexpected bonus.
So they ashed the fields
of Auschwitz, four feet deep
around the chutes.

Busy with my new voice
and far, far away,
I never heard the cries.
The smell, like burnt chicken,
some say, diffused before
it reached me, raptly
experimenting with gravity
in a crib big as a house.

Yet those days became my Grimm
and Andersen, subliminal
and magnified from the originals:
my ogre eats whole towns,
my wicked witch puts neighborhoods
of children into her oven,
and my brave woodsman arrives
too late. When he cuts open
the wolf, he finds only mountains
of spectacles, hair, and winter coats.

Home Front

It must have been '45, a backyard spring,
about the time my father's regiment moved
through Buchenwald, when hollyhocks, yellow,
white, lavender, still opened every morning
to the clatter of trash cans in the alley
sloping behind our garage, where the alley kids
waited with grudges carried like impetigo,
where the little one with the built-up sole
bloodied my nose one winter afternoon,
and again when I donned the Nazi pilot's gloves
my father shipped from Cologne with the picture
of himself sitting proud in his new moustache
that Mother said made him look like Stalin,
gloves with the smell of war, long canvas mitts
that reached above my elbows, with trigger fingers,
the sight of which should have warned Soldier
to any alley kid. When I finished crying,
Mother washed my face and took me to the Uptown
for Hitler ducks surprised by G.I. pigeons
and *The Fighting Sullivans*. It must have been
after that winter, in '45, when the grocer
everybody called Cousin Bob, who sold
Grapette and jaw breakers in his basement store
at the end of Cedar Street and had a gold star
hung in his front door window for a son
burned over Regensberg, would rock in his porch swing
all Sunday beside his radio and a pitcher
of "iced tea," Mother said. It had to be then,
when *Life* and *Movietone* still brought weekly news
of my father and the others driving deep
into the Reich's dark forests, that Cousin Bob,
the big pitcher sweating beside him, called me up
on his porch and told me this: if you walk down

alone by the Jewish cemetery near nightfall,
just before the crickets start, you can hear
the old rabbis in their long gray beards
snoring away. "They go, 'Jeeeeeeeewwwww,'"
he said, and burst out laughing.

Sunday School Lesson
from Capt. Daniel Mayhew,
USAAF, Ret.

Big voiced, G.I. husky, he strained
his civies at the shoulders—a man
too broad for the stuff our fathers wore.
He let Moses rattle on and Job contemplate
the new boil on his forehead. In their place,
he gave us Schweinfurt, Regensburg, Ploesti:
Dekker's crew bailing out, one by one,
till five were counted, the other five
augering in on one wing and a black
smear of burning fuel. On the day
he had to jump, the blow of sky ripped
off a glove with his wedding ring inside:
"A kind of prophecy," he said, smiling.

We, his puppy crew, saw it fall,
put ourselves, our desks in the ready room
before dawn, getting briefed for the day's
high chase across the Rhine, knowing
it would always be the other guy, the loner,
bed-wetter from Detroit, or was it Trenton?

—all this till the day his big hands
began to shake, the amazing tears welled,
and he stood up, saying, "We're having
fun, aren't we, you silly little shits."

The next Sunday, Miss Branson read to us
of Lot, God's grief, and the burning cities.

G.I. Joe from Kokomo

All this has given rise today
to the idea, particularly among the
veterans of the Vietnam War, that
World War II should be thought of as
a good war, a "pure" war.
        James Jones

Somehow he's become a friendly uncle: bachelor,
born storyteller, who stops in unannounced
for chitchat and a beer, who still smokes
Luckies, lights them with an agate-smooth Zippo
he's carried since Fort Sill. Forty years
ago, dizzy and quick with fear, he carried it
to Utah Beach, bent on living if he could
or dying bravely if he had to. A gangly eagle
scout in love with fair play and allegiance,
he waded past a dozen buddies already
bobbing in the surf, staggered for cover in historical
black and white till crowds pressed in
to see the fire boats plume him back from Victory.
Only now and then does he forget
and let the dead hand show, its finger
sprouting a yellow talon, hard as bone.
Twenty-one again this June, he plans
to marry, study law, then run for office.

JAMES TATE
(1943–)

The Lost Pilot

for my father, 1922–1944

Your face did not rot
like the others—the co-pilot,
for example, I saw him

yesterday. His face is corn-
mush: his wife and daughter,
the poor ignorant people, stare

as if he will compose soon.
He was more wronged than Job.
But your face did not rot

like the others—it grew dark,
and hard like ebony;
the features progressed in their

distinction. If I could cajole
you to come back for an evening,
down from your compulsive

orbiting, I would touch you,
read your face as Dallas,
your hoodlum gunner, now,

with the blistered eyes, reads
his braille editions. I would
touch your face as a disinterested

scholar touches an original page.
However frightening, I would
discover you, and I would not

turn you in; I would not make
you face your wife, or Dallas,
or the co-pilot, Jim. You

could return to your crazy
orbiting, and I would not try
to fully understand what

it means to you. All I know
is this: when I see you,
as I have seen you at least

once every year of my life,
spin across the wilds of the sky
like a tiny, African god,

I feel dead. I feel as if I were
the residue of a stranger's life,
that I should pursue you.

My head cocked toward the sky,
I cannot get off the ground,
and, you, passing over again,

fast, perfect, and unwilling
to tell me that you are doing
well, or that it was mistake

that placed you in that world,
and me in this; or that misfortune
placed these worlds in us.

DOROTHY COFFIN SUSSMAN

(1945–)

Coming Home

The day before my father came home from the war
my mother waxed the floors, and in their wide oak boards
saw her own smiling face. Reckless,
she polished anything that would take a shine.
At the clothesline she beat the parlor rug to death
and felt the breath of the Colorado Rockies graze her neck.
Her body swayed as if my father were already
running his hands over her, whispering *my girl*
of the western slope into her hungry mouth,
as if she were singing *Oh Johnny, How You Can Love,* into his.

She moved through the hum and swirl and press of the day,
her hands busy in vinegar wash.
In late afternoon she ironed sheets. She took her time,
lifted the new cotton to her face, took in the dizzying mix
of soap and bleach. She watched steam rise
off the cloth, imagined him, them, dazed and lost in that tangle of
        white.

She didn't think then that in time the cloth would wear out,
couldn't know she'd wear so far down. Looking back
she'd say those first days were their happiest, before the booze,
and she'd come to wonder what she could have done
to free the man who came back to her a stranger,
a man locked in nightmares.

And when there was nothing left to dust or wash or wax or sweep
        away,
my mother scoured her own body, dipped her hair in lemon juice,
coiled the strands to pincurls and lay down naked

beside the bed, the hairpins a pillow of nails,
and waited for my father to come home.

* * *

In another house now, my mother dreams West.
She stands in her kitchen at dusk and plays old cowboy songs
on the phonograph and dances the Colorado shuffle alone.
She hears Johnny's boozy snore drop from the room above
and she turns up the music. She longs to rock
her children, now grown and gone,
who have children of their own.
When they call she tells them she's fine
and that when she wins the lottery she'll buy a Cadillac
and pile everyone in the car and zoom out to Colorado
and let them see with their own eyes what real mountains are.

She'll become thin again, and beautiful. Her hair
that's gone brittle and gray will be the soft golden blonde
Johnny once loved, especially that night she swept
it off her neck and pinned its damp luxury on top of her head.
She'll wait for Johnny to come down from the mountains
and they'll start over, out there where there's room,
out there with a sky so deep and close it has to be heaven.

River Stories

Weepy drunk, Christmas Eve, 1988, my father in his steamy
    kitchen
honorably discharged from the U.S. Army in 1945,
is telling river stories to my brothers
who've heard them all a hundred times:
how his 96th Mountain Division skied into Italy
and took it from the Dagos and the Krauts.

He stands at the butcher block and makes quick cuts
in the black skin of olives, chops three toes of garlic
into hot oil, and my mother says, "He's a genius, your dad,
making something out of nothing," and I
think, *It's only spaghetti sauce,* and how
hard she must work to believe anything these days.

He talks about schusshing along the Po,
the only sound, men moving across the snow,
the sound that could have been the wind,
or maybe not your own men, and how hard
you learned to listen for the difference.
And how deep the river froze that last winter.

His knife glitters silver in the flourescent light.
My mother's arms stiffen across her chest—"Let it go,"
she says, "it was just a river. For once in your life
say so!" She buries her face in her apron:
Her shoulders heave, but no sounds come.

My brothers take her from the room.
I wait for them to come back. I wait,
as I have waited all my life, for my father
to tell the true story in front of us—the one he relived
in their bedroom, the one I could never quite make out,
night after night through those nightmare years.

"No one ever comes back the same," he says.

Across forty years of freeze and thaw, I see
the rifle butt digging a grave in his shoulder.
I see him hiding in a deep pine forest
waxing his heavy oak skis, then
whipping along that solid river like a hawk.

I see what his knife could do,
finding a throat, the carotid's knotty pulse.
I see him loosening the blood from its banks,
hear the neckbones crack, the sound
scattering across the snow. I hear it all.

R. S. GWYNN
(1948–)

Randolph Field, 1938

Hands of men blasted the world asunder;
How they lived God only knew!
If you'd live to be a gray haired wonder,
Keep the nose out of the blue!

Framed by the open window, a lone Stearman
Wobbles, dips right, dips left, then dives and banks
For touch-and-go, seeming barely to miss
The sunlit "Taj Mahal" and a stray egret
Who has mistaken grass and shimmering concrete
For salt marsh. Two flies on the windowsill
Wait for their chance. The wind-sock hangs limp
In the thick heat, and lunch has not been cleared.

Indeed, the messtray resting on the nightstand
Has not been touched, or hardly—half a weiner,
Succotash and boiled carrots stirred around,
Even the tea and gingerbread just tasted,
And the young man there who has no appetite
Has raised himself up from the sweaty pillow
To watch some fledgling's first attempt, as stirring
As a scene from *The West Point of the Air.*

It slips from sight. He leans his head back, dizzy
From the slight effort, shuddering against
The squeal of tires, the buzz-saw radial engine
Over-throttled, straining up to a stall,
And then, the day's sole miracle, the steady
Hum of the prop—somebody else's luck.
For now the chills have come to spike his fever,
Everything holding true to course but him.

The skinny nurse who takes his temperature
Charts the latest, 102.8,
And then connects the dots with a red line
That climbs and plummets like a rookie's struggle
To keep the nose cowl flush with the horizon.
It would be funny, but it simply isn't,
Even when Szulic and Rosenthal, his buddies,
Saunter in after class with cokes and Luckies.

He'll envy them that night when, after supper,
He lies in bed and smokes. It isn't easy
To think of them with girls along the River—
Dancehalls, music, beer, all with such sweetness
In the mild evening air he'd like to cry.
He has missed the chance, like Aaron Rosenthal,
To burn above Berlin; like Thomas Szulic,
To spin in wingless somewhere over France.

A decade and a war still to be crossed
Before he is my father, he is only
One of the Dodos, barely voting age,
Washed out a week before he gets his wings.
A radio is playing now. Kay Kyser.
. . . *To be in Carolina in the mornin'* . . .
It's hard to think of what he must go back to.
He banked on everything but going back.

Off to the southeast, thunderheads are building—
Heat lightning flashing like imagined guns,
Faint thunder and a breeze that brings the Gulf
Into this place of starched white sheets and Lysol
Where he lies watching three red points of light,
A late flight coming in for night approach.
He shuts his eyes and tries to think of nothing
Before he sideslips into dreams of fire.

DAVID BOTTOMS
(1949–)

The Anniversary

This is the night I come to my room,
a bottle of brandy, or whiskey, a glass,
and close the door on the rest of the house,
pull the shades, switch off the lights,
imagine a darkness just as it may have been.
I pull my chair to the middle of the room,
fall to it like a man with a mission,
and do not turn on the radio, the stereo,
as I might do on any other night,
but listen to the pines brush the house
with a sound like the bow of a ship
rising and falling through water.
Then I drink for the shakes and I get them
when I see again jarring the darkness
the terrible rising sun, the searchlight
of the *Hiei* stabbing across the sound,
and jolt in my chair as the turret slues,
guns already deafening the long light blind.
Look, there he is at the door of the turret
and then, God, the blast of the shell
kicks him right back out! Then, God . . .
what? For this is the night my father,
forehead shattered, side pierced, was thrown
for dead from the deck of the *Atlanta*,
toward a place that was not Guadalcanal
or Florida Island, drifted like a man dead
to the world ending around him, and was dead
to the arms of the sailors in the lifeboat,
dead as any drunk in any armchair
who trembles at the horror of his thoughts
and learns, as he learns every year,

that the power in the blood to terrify
is sometimes the power of love. So moves
one knee trembling toward his desk,
stands on shaky legs and puts down his glass,
leans on the desk and opens the drawer,
feels for the small pearl-handled knife,
the sharpest blade of Japanese steel,
This is your blood in remembrance of you,
who died one night at sea and lived,
brings it to his face, brings it to his eye,
touches with the nervous point
the flesh of his forehead, an old scar.

EDWARD HIRSCH

(1950–)

Leningrad (1941–1943)

1

For some of us it began with wild dogs
Howling like dirges in the early morning
And crazed wolves answering in the distance.

It began with the shrieking of peacocks
And three mad sables roving through the streets
And a sound of donkeys screeching like children.

Some of us heard the polar bears wailing
And two African giraffes whining in terror
At the death throes of a baby elephant

And we knew it had begun in earnest.
But some people refuse to imagine zebras
Careening around in hysterical circles,

Or cheetahs smashing their cages, or bats
Clinging to crippled leopards and then
Floating over their heads in a broad light.

Some people need to see the sky speaking
German, and the night wearing a steel helmet,
And the moon slowly turning into a swastika.

2

But then we saw the stomach of the city
Burning in the distance, all the charred
Sugar and fresh meats, all the white flour

And dark grains flaming on the far horizon
In oily black clouds of smoke tinged
With ember-reds and soiled brown mauves.

It was like seeing hundreds of waves of
Blood rolling over the city at dusk and then
Hanging in heavy layers under the stars.

No one cried out or screamed in pain
To see our crumbling wooden depots of food
Climbing in swollen clouds into the sky

But a few children who were already hungry
And an old man who saw his own small intestine
Drifting like a balloon over his wife's head.

That's how in Peter the Great's white showcase
Built on a vast swamp on the northernmost
Fringe of Europe, we began to starve.

3

It's to lie in the dark at four a.m.
Thinking about the sweetness of surrender,
What the mind yields to a mattress in fatigue

And the body forgets to remember, what
The reluctant night yields to a cold room
Where windows are boarded with plywood

And light searches for a crack in the roof.
It's to remember the women with bright parasols
Strolling down the wide Parisian boulevards

And the men cruising in black limousines.
It's to forget the words "typhoid" and "cholera,"
The sirens that go on wailing in your sleep.

There are days when dying will seem as
Easy as sitting down in a warm, comfortable
Overstuffed chair and going back to sleep,

Or lying in bed for hours. But you must
Not sit down, you must spend your life digging
Out trenches with a shovel, staying awake.

4

So whoever will eat must work and whoever
Will survive must fight. But the sick
Civilians shiver on narrow gray stretchers

In the dark in unheated hospital rooms,
The soldiers respect the terror of their wounds.
There is no water, no warmth, and no light

And the bodies keep piling up in the corridor.
A red soldier tears his mouth from a bandage
And announces to a young nurse, "Darling,

Tanks are what we need now, beautiful tanks,
Beloved tanks rolling over the barren fields
And playing their music in the pink sky."

No one pays attention, but a volunteer regrets
That trolleys have stopped running to the front:
He'll have to walk the distance. Meanwhile,

The bodies keep piling up in the corridor
And a dazed girl keeps shouting, "But I *can*
Fight the Nazis!" Whoever can fight will eat.

5

I have lanced the boils on every finger
And sucked the warm pus; I have eaten
A thin jelly made of leather straps,

And swallowed the acrid green oil cakes,
And tasted a cold extract of pine needles.
I have stared at the flayed white trees

And watched my children chasing a scrawny
Cat through the streets at dawn, and smelled
The dead cat boiling in my own kitchen.

I have tried to relinquish judgment,
To eat the cat or the dog without disgust.
I have seen starved women begging for rations

And starved men crawling under a frozen black
Sun, and I have turned my back slowly.
I have waited in a thousand lines for bread,

But I won't gouge at another human body;
I won't eat the sweet breasts of a murdered
Woman, or the hacked thighs of a dying man.

6

After we burned the furniture and the books
In the stove, we were always cold, always:
But we got used to icicles in our chests.

We got used to the fires falling from the sky
At dusk, spreading across the scorched roofs.
And we got used to the formula of edible

Cellulose and cottonseed cakes and dry meal dust
And a pinch of corn flour for our dark bread.
We got used to our own stomachs bulging with air.

And then one day the bodies started to appear
Piled on the bright sleds of little children,
Bundled up in thick curtains and torn sheets

And old rags and sometimes even in newspapers.
We saw the staircases jammed with corpses,
The doorways and the dead-end alleys, and smelled

A scent of turpentine hanging in the frosty air.
We got used to leaving our dead unburied,
Stacked like cordwood in the drifts of snow.

7

Somehow we lived with our empty stomachs
And our ankles in chains, somehow we managed
With a heavy iron collar wrapped tightly

Around our necks. Sometimes the sun seemed
Like a German bomber, or an air-raid warden,
Or a common foot soldier speaking German.

We saw houses that had been sliced in two
From the attic to the cellar and large buildings
That had been blown apart like small windows.

We saw a soldier cradling a kneecap in his palms
And children watching the soft red fluids
Of their intestines flowing through their fingers.

We saw a girl tearing out clumps of hair
And surgeons who tried to scratch out their eyes
Because they couldn't stand to see their hands.

Slowly we touched a sharp razor to our necks
And scraped away the useless blue skin
And the dead flesh. Somehow we lived.

ANDREW HUDGINS

(1951–)

Air View of an Industrial Scene

There is a train at the ramp, unloading people
who stumble from the cars and toward the gate.
The building's shadows tilt across the ground
and from each shadow juts a longer one
and from that shadow crawls a shadow of smoke
black as just-plowed earth. Inside the gate
is a small garden and someone on his knees.
Perhaps he's fingering the yellow blooms
to see which ones have set and will soon wither,
clinging to a green tomato as it swells.
The people hold back, but are forced to the open gate,
and when they enter they will see the garden
and some, gardeners themselves, will yearn
to fall to their knees there, untangling vines,
plucking at weeds, cooling their hands in damp earth.
They're going to die soon, a matter of minutes.
Even from our height, we see in the photograph
the shadow of the plane stamped dark and large
on Birkenau, one black wing shading the garden.
We can't tell which are guards, which prisoners.
We're watchers. But if we had bombs we'd drop them.

MARY JO SALTER
(1954–)

Welcome to Hiroshima

is what you first see, stepping off the train:
a billboard brought to you in living English
by Toshiba Electric. While a channel
silent in the TV of the brain

projects those flickering re-runs of a cloud
that brims its risen columnful like beer
and, spilling over, hangs its foamy head,
you feel a thirst for history: what year

it started to be safe to breathe the air,
and when to drink the blood and scum afloat
on the Ohta River. But no, the water's clear,
they pour it for your morning cup of tea

in one of the countless sunny coffee shops
whose plastic dioramas advertise
mutations of cuisine behind the glass:
a pancake sandwich; a pizza someone tops

with a maraschino cherry. Passing by
the Peace Park's floral hypocenter (where
how bravely, or with what mistaken cheer,
humanity erased its own erasure),

you enter the memorial museum
and through more glass are served, as on a dish
of blistered grass, three mannequins. Like gloves
a mother clips to coatsleeves, strings of flesh

hang from their fingertips; or as if tied
to recall a duty for us, *Reverence
the dead whose mourners too shall soon be dead,*
but all commemoration's swallowed up

in questions of bad taste, how re-created
horror mocks the grim original,
and thinking at last *They should have left it all*
you stop. This is the wristwatch of a child.

Jammed on the moment's impact, resolute
to communicate some message, although mute,
it gestures with its hands at eight-fifteen
and eight-fifteen and eight-fifteen again

while tables of statistics on the wall
update the news by calling on a roll
of tape, death gummed on death, and in the case
adjacent, an exhibit under glass

is glass itself: a shard the bomb slammed in
a woman's arm at eight-fifteen, but some
three decades on—as if to make it plain
hope's only as renewable as pain,

and as if all the unsung
debasements of the past may one day come
rising to the surface once again—
worked its filthy way out like a tongue.

P. H. LIOTTA
(1956–)

The Story I Can't Tell

I

Forty-three years ago today,
Stuart James is climbing
to 30,000 feet, heading
out of the horizon
from East Anglia on a clear,
faultlessly blue day in a war
so long ago we pretend
to barely hear its echoes.
We are near the lead of this V
formation of 230 B-17
flying fortresses, the drone
of our own four engines
struggling and humming
with vibration, living up
to our name for this nightmare
christened *Banshee*. There are
twelve of us on board. I'm here
because the stupid copilot
got his head sheared off
over the coast near Abbeville, when
the Focke-Wulfs split-S'ed out of heaven,
where their bullets pierced the bullet-
proof plexiglass and wedged a clean
red streak across his throat.
There's the navigator,
engineer, and bombardier;
five gunners for high,
tail, turret, and waist—where
Jack Martin, 17, is missing

two fingers on his left hand,
souvenirs of victory
over Hamburg two years back. He
remembers watching them break off
in the slipstream of fifty below
zero, while he wouldn't quit firing
and sweating, tumbling like spent
cartridges back to earth six miles
down. There's our talisman
named Faustus, jet-black cat;
we'd never live a flight
without him. And then there's you,
Stuart: aircraft commander, at
21 the Old Man on the crew,
veteran of 8 missions, and though
I won't be born for another
decade, you look the way
I've always known you: old and sad.
Even the oxygen mask
can't stop the possibility
of a smile just beginning to
suggest itself behind your steel-
rimmed glasses in those dumb,
confused blue eyes. I know this.
Time means nothing and everything
in this story, Stuart, and today
I am wiser than you because
I know what is going to happen.
It is February 13th, 1945. We are
heading east to Dresden.

                                         But we will never
see that bright city novaed
into flames nearly 60,000
feet high. We see only Messerschmitts
pour out of the sun like black flies.
We feel the sky rain with steel
splinters. The flak pops in dull
black puffs of breath
around us. Ships blown apart:
their wings ground to powder;
wounds open in their sides

as flames stream out behind;
diving or stalling or spinning
out of the air, pieces of them
drifting past, now chunks of metal
with men inside, with names like
Memphis Belle, Vertical Shaft,
Dog Breath, Idiot's Delight, Arise
My Love and Come with Me,
100 yards to the right you wave
to Joe Beebe, pilot of *Death from*
Above; he's looking right at you
and starts to wave back, and then
he's gone, half of the airplane missing.
You hear his voice, like the lathered
breath of a horse, scream
of fire in his oxygen tanks; you
hear him burned alive.
                              And when
your turn comes, the flak rips through
the bomb bay doors. The sound of
a train roaring behind you is only
the wind at three hundred knots.
Holding the shuddering
control of the flight column, you hear
the bombardier scream *Salvo*
the load! as you ask for a drop
zone. As you fall through the clouds,
rapidly losing altitude, you see
the copilot's eyes filled
with their own light, feel the red
shrapnel perforate your cheek and
the open hole your tongue plays with.
You know that you will not die,
but something is wrong.
Perhaps it is the sudden frenzy
of a voice which says *Now!*
Perhaps it is something in you
when you order the jettison
of the incendiary white phos-
phorous. Perhaps it is the screams
of wild gratitude from the crew

as you bank high and left, when
you see that heaven is as much
a lie as this life, while we watch
these little candles from hell
which do not drop
like beautiful, graceful flowers,
but fall like bombs to blossom
in brilliant orange along the cob-
bled pavement of a hamlet
on the lee side of a mountain.

II

For years you woke from the chalice
of dream, still able to see the
tears of flame lining the village
streets, and the transfigured bodies
dance like butterflies as the
canisters of flaming liquid burst
behind them. You woke from the film
of sweat, whispering the names
of those no one remembers, seeing
their deaths and the day you killed them:
a child's face punctured with glass;
flesh runs off her skull like syrup.

Now you no longer wake and the
innocence is gone from your eyes.
Now only your breath rises
in the autumnal host of air
which smells like ether. Now, Stuart,
only your voice remains where the in-
visible tongue of the wind
unfurls the shape of your words,
and blows them back, it tells you
Nothing

It's a story
only you can tell of how
it's always an accident:

the way we fall back
into the past or feel
the burning of a future
none of us prepared to enter.

Notes on the Poets

W. H. Auden (1907–1973). One of the twentieth century's greatest poets, Auden was born in England but moved to the United States in 1939. He became a United States citizen in 1946.

Donald W. Baker (1923–). Baker served as a navigator on a bomber during the war. He taught for many years at Wabash College and is now retired and living on Cape Cod. In 1985 he published *Unposted Letters*.

John Berryman (1914–1972). Considered one of the principal members of the confessional school of poetry in the 1960s, Berryman is known primarily for his long, personal group of poems gathered under the title *The Dream Songs*.

David Bottoms (1949–). Both novelist and poet, Bottoms's most recent book of poems is *Under the Vulture-Tree*. He teaches creative writing at Georgia State University.

Edgar Bowers (1924–). Bowers served in the U.S. Army from 1943 through 1946. He has taught for many years at the University of California, Santa Barbara. His most recent book is *For Louis Pasteur* from Princeton University Press.

Van K. Brock (1932–). Raised in southern Georgia, Brock is co-director of the creative writing program at Florida State University in Tallahassee. He has written many poems on the Nazi phenomenon and the holocaust.

Turner Cassity (1929–). Cassity's latest book is *Hurricane Lamp*, from the University of Chicago Press. He has worked in the Emory University Library in Atlanta since 1962.

JOHN CIARDI (1916–1986). Ciardi served as a gunner on a B-29 stationed on the island of Saipan, in the South Pacific, with the Army Air Force during World War II. During his life, he achieved fame as a poet, translator, editor, teacher, critic, and lexicographer.

E. E. CUMMINGS (1894–1962). After several shattering experiences during World War I, Cummings became a pacifist and iconoclast for the remainder of his life. His poetry, among the most idiosyncratic and innovative of the twentieth century, stands as a tribute to the individual mind and to the life lived by passion.

JAMES DICKEY (1923–). Winner of the National Book Award for Poetry, Dickey also served as consultant in poetry to the Library of Congress for two terms. He is the author of the novel *Deliverance* and is currently poet in residence and Carolina Professor at the University of South Carolina.

ALAN DUGAN (1923–). Dugan served with the Army Air Force in World War II. His first book of poetry, *Poems,* was awarded the Yale Series of Younger Poets Award, the Pulitzer Prize, the National Book Award, and the Prix de Rome.

RICHARD EBERHART (1904–). Eberhart was an aerial gunnery officer in the navy during World War II. He has received many honors for his poetry. In 1978 he was declared poet laureate of the state of New Hampshire.

WILLIAM EVERSON (1912–). Drafted as a conscientious objector in 1943, William Everson spent the Second World War in various work camps. Although linked with the beat generation of the 1950s, he became a Dominican monk and published much of his work under the name Brother Antoninus.

EDWARD FIELD (1924–). Field's first book was awarded the Lamont Poetry Award in 1962. Since then Field has published many volumes, as well as editing the popular poetry anthology *A Geography of Poets.* During World War II, he served as navigator in a bomber in the European theater.

R. S. GWYNN (1948–). Gywnn's first book, *The Drive-In,* was published by the University of Missouri Press as winner of the

Breakthrough Award. Gwynn teaches creative writing at Lamar University in Beaumont, Texas.

DONALD HALL (1928–). The winner of numerous awards for his poetry, Donald Hall is also the author of several textbooks about poetry and other language-related matters. A former teacher of creative writing at the University of Michigan, Hall has retired to Eagle Pond Farm near Danbury, New Hampshire, to write full time.

ROBERT HAYDEN (1918–1980). Born in Detroit, Hayden studied at the University of Michigan. He taught for many years at Fisk University in Nashville, then returned to his alma mater, where he taught until his death. He won several awards for his poetry.

ANTHONY HECHT (1923–). Winner of the Pulitzer Prize for poetry in 1968, Anthony Hecht often writes about the darkest and most disturbing events in the history of Western civilization and the twentieth century in particular. During World War II, he joined the army and served in both Europe and Japan.

EDWARD HIRSCH (1950–). A recent winner of the Prix de Rome, Hirsch teaches creative writing at the University of Houston. His most recent book of poems is The Night Parade from Knopf.

ANDREW HUDGINS (1951–). Raised in the South, Hudgins now teaches at the University of Cincinnati. His most recent book is After the Lost War, a book of poems about the Civil War and its aftermath, centering around the life of Sidney Lanier.

RICHARD HUGO (1923–1982). During World War II, Hugo flew thirty-five missions as a bombardier in Italy for the Army Air Force. After the war he studied with Theodore Roethke at the University of Washington. His poetry often focuses on the Pacific Northwest, where Hugo lived most of his life. He is considered one of the great regional poets of this century.

RANDALL JARRELL (1914–1965). Jarrell enlisted in the Army Air Corps in World War II and served as a control-tower operator working with B-29 crews. His war poetry is among the most powerful literary documents to come out of the Second World War.

ROBINSON JEFFERS (1887–1962). Jeffers was one of the few poets to oppose the United States' entrance into the Second World War. His poetry and his life were immersed in nature and the environment he found along the California coast near Carmel. He regarded the urban and mechanized lives of most people in the twentieth century as "against nature."

WELDON KEES (1914–1955). A mysterious figure whose poetry was not well known during his lifetime, Kees disappeared in San Francisco in 1955 and has not been heard from since.

LINCOLN KIRSTEIN (1907–). Kirstein joined the army in 1943. He was attached to the arts, monuments, and archives section of Gen. George Patton's Third Army. Unlike the other poets in this anthology, Kirstein's wartime experiences provide the major theme of his poetry. After the war, he served for many years as director of the New York City Ballet Company.

P. H. LIOTTA (1956–). Liotta's poems have appeared in many periodicals, including *Poetry* magazine. Liotta lives in Palmer Lake, Colorado, and teaches creative writing at the United States Air Force Academy.

ROBERT LOWELL (1917–1977). Lowell was a conscientious objector during the Second World War. One of the most honored poets of the second half of this century, Lowell is known for poetry characterized by an often extremely personal subject matter and tone that, in his best poems, creates an art of great power.

ARCHIBALD MACLEISH (1892–1982). MacLeish served as a captain of field artillery in World War I. In 1939, he was appointed Librarian of Congress and served in this post until 1944, when he was appointed Assistant Secretary of State until Roosevelt's death. He also served during the war as director of the Office of Facts and Figures. He won the Pulitzer Prize for both poetry and drama.

WALTER MCDONALD (1934–). McDonald is director of the creative writing program at Texas Tech University. From 1957 to 1971 he was a United States Air Force pilot and flew bombing missions in Vietnam. Among his many books is *After the Noise of Saigon*.

PHYLLIS MCGINLEY (1905–1978). Known primarily as a writer of children's stories, McGinley also published several books of poetry and was awarded the Pulitzer Prize in 1961 for *Times Three.*

WILLIAM MEREDITH (1919–). William Meredith spent most of the Second World War as a naval aviator in the Pacific. His poetry is characterized by a great craftmanship and delicate sense of control. He is chancellor of the Academy of American Poets.

JOHN N. MILLER (1933–). John Miller lived in Hawaii from 1937 to 1951 and was on the Mamakua Coast of the Big Island when Pearl Harbor was attacked. He presently teaches English at Denison University in Granville, Ohio.

MARIANNE MOORE (1887–1972). A true original, Moore has turned her creative mind to many subjects during her career. Her work is often filled with an unpretentious wit and humor, even when she is addressing subjects others might find somber.

HOWARD NEMEROV (1920–). Nemerov first joined the Canadian Air Force in World War II and flew combat missions against the Germans. He later served in the United States Army Air Corps from 1943 to 1945. He teaches at Washington University in St. Louis, Missouri. His *Collected Poems* was awarded the Pulitzer Prize and the National Book Award in 1978. He served as poet laureate of the United States in 1989 and 1990.

KENNETH PATCHEN (1911–1972). For many years a central force in the world of poetry on the American west coast, Patchen published unorthodox, often comic verse. *The Collected Poems of Kenneth Patchen* was published by New Direction in 1968.

GIBBONS RUARK (1941–). Ruark teaches English at the University of Delaware. He has made numerous trips abroad, particularly to Ireland and Italy, often the subjects of his poetry. His most recent books are *Keeping Company* and *Small Rain.*

LARRY RUBIN (1930–). Rubin is a professor of English at Georgia Institute of Technology in Atlanta. His most recent book of poems is *All My Mirrors Lie.*

MARY JO SALTER (1954–). The author of two books of poetry, Salter writes poetry distinguished by its formal excellence. She was awarded the Lamont Poetry Prize in 1989.

MAY SARTON (1912–). Sarton was born in Belgium and became a United States citizen in 1924. During World War II, she taught English at Harvard University. Her *Collected Poems* was published in 1974, and she lives presently in York, Maine.

WINFIELD TOWNLEY SCOTT (1910–1968). Scott worked as a journalist on the staff of *The Providence Journal* during the Second World War. His *Collected Poems* was published shortly before his death.

KARL SHAPIRO (1913–). One of the most popular American war poets during World War II and immediately after, Shapiro wrote the well-received *V-Letter* in 1945, for which he won the Pulitzer Prize. He has since published many books, including *Selected Poems*, which won the Bollingen Prize in 1968.

LOUIS SIMPSON (1923–). Simpson was born in the British West Indies and became an American citizen as a young man. During the war he served as part of a tank corps and in the infantry of the 101st Airborne Division. His poetry was awarded the Pulitzer Prize in 1964. He teaches at the State University of New York at Stony Brook.

W. D. SNODGRASS (1926–). Snodgrass served with the navy in the Pacific during the last year of World War II. His first book, *Heart's Needle,* was awarded the Pulitzer Prize in 1960, primarily for the groundbreaking accomplishment of its title poem. Since then, he has published several books, including *The Fuhrer Bunker.* He teaches at the University of Delaware.

LUCIEN STRYK (1924–). The author of many books on Zen Buddhism as well as poetry, Stryk's *Collected Poems* was published in 1984 by Ohio University Press. He teaches at Northern Illinois University.

DOROTHY COFFIN SUSSMAN (1945–). Dorothy Sussman was born in Colorado and grew up in Schuylerville, New York. She is completing her last year of study in the master of fine arts program in creative writing at Georgia State University.

JAMES TATE (1943–). Tate's first book, *The Lost Pilot*, was awarded the Yale Series of Younger Poets Award in 1966. He teaches in the creative writing program at the University of Massachusetts in Amherst.

WILLIAM TROWBRIDGE (1941–). Trowbridge published his first full collection of poetry, *Enter Dark Stranger*, with the University of Arkansas Press in 1989.

PETER VIERECK (1916–). Viereck was, for many years, professor of modern history at Mt. Holyoke College. His first book of poems, *Terror and Decorum*, won the Pulitzer Prize in 1949. He has also published extensively in political science and history.

JAMES WHITEHEAD (1936–). Whitehead grew up in Mississippi. He is the author of two books of poetry, *Domains* and *Local Men*, from the University of Illinois Press, as well as a chapbook entitled *Actual Size*. He teaches in the creative writing program at the University of Arkansas.

REED WHITTEMORE (1919–). Whittemore has published his witty and often humorous poetry in many volumes over the years. He has taught for many of those years at the University of Maryland.

RICHARD WILBUR (1921–). One of America's most renowned and honored poets and translators, Wilbur was awarded both the Pulitzer Prize and the National Book Award in 1956 for his book *Things of This World* and he won a second Pulitzer Prize in 1989 for his *New and Collected Poems*. He served as poet laureate of the United States in 1988.

C. K. WILLIAMS (1936–). C. K. Williams's poetry often deals directly with the most serious atrocities of twentieth-century life. His unflinching look at himself and the world around him has gained him a devoted following among readers of poetry. He spends much of his time in France but also teaches at George Mason University.

MILLER WILLIAMS (1930–). Miller Williams has published many books of poetry as well as translations. His work has won many awards, including the Prix de Rome. His most recent book is *Living on the Surface: New and Selected Poems*, from Louisiana State University Press.

INDEX

DATE DUE
